Ultimate Love

NEIL T. ANDERSON
DAVE PARK

HARVEST HOUSE PUBLISHERS
Eugene, Oregon 97402

Cover design by Garborg Design Works, Minneapolis, Minnesota

Illustrations by Scott Angle

ULTIMATE LOVE

Copyright © 1996 by Harvest House Publishers
Eugene, Oregon 97402

ISBN 1-56507-410-6

Printed in the United States of America.

96 97 98 99 00 01 02 03 /BC/ 10 9 8 7 6 5 4 3 2 1

Acknowledgments and Dedication

We want to thank all the staff at Freedom in Christ Ministries.

To the whole Harvest House team, thanks for loving youth and caring enough about them to provide valuable resources that direct them to their freedom in Christ.

This book is dedicated to Ashley and Dani Park and to Heidi Anderson, our daughters. As your fathers we've watched you grow. You're not as small as you once were. We hope and pray that you will walk free in Christ all the days of your life and experience His matchless love and acceptance. We also pray that as your dads we will model that love and acceptance for you. Ashley, Dani, and Heidi, we love you.

Contents

The 10-40 Challenge

We've all been told to break a habit. But not all habits are bad. We hope you've already established the good habit of being in God's Word daily. But if you haven't, that's what this book is all about. We hope you'll take the 10-40 Challenge. What is the 10-40 Challenge? It's simple:

Take at least 10 minutes a day
for
40 days.

Spend at least 10 minutes in God's Word each day for 40 days, then see if you haven't developed the habit of getting into God's Word on a regular basis.

> I, _____, accept the *10-40 Challenge* to develop the awesome habit of meeting daily with God.
>
> Today's date: _____.

This book, *Ultimate Love,* is part of a devotional series titled *Freedom in Christ for Teens.* If you haven't gone through book number one, *Extreme Faith,* or book number two, *Reality Check,* you may want to consider going through them first. These devotionals lay down the important foundation of our identity in Christ and how to win the battle for your mind. Then don't stop there! Check out the devotional book *Awesome God.*

How To Use This Book

1. First, pray against the enemy and pray for God's understanding.
2. Take the time to spot the key verses used each day. Look them up in your Bible to catch the context.
3. Look up and read each of the Scripture references given, then write out your personal comment and insights about them.
4. Answer each of the "Love Lesson" questions from your own perspective, as they relate to your own life.
5. State out loud the lie to reject and the truth to accept as well as the other statements you're asked to say out loud.
6. Monitor your progress by using the 40-day checklist.

Try to find a quiet place and specific time to meet with God daily. Make sure there are no interruptions and distractions (like the TV or radio) to bug you. Ezra 7:10 says, "Ezra had devoted himself to the study and observance of the Law of the LORD, and to teaching its decrees and laws in Israel."

Find someone to be accountable to, like a trusted friend, youth pastor, brother, or sister (maybe even your mom or dad). Ask them to monitor your progress at least once a week.

My accountability partner is
(name):

We will meet every
(select a day of the week):

_____

40-day checklist: Check off each day as you complete it and monitor your progress. It would be a good idea to select one verse from each chapter to memorize that week. Pick the verse or verses that speak to you, the ones you sense that God would have you hide in your heart.

40-Day Checklist

1. His Love Is Love   Date completed: _____
2. The Greatest Act of Love Date completed: _____
3. A Touch of His Love Date completed: _____
4. He Calls Us Friend   Date completed: _____
5. Loving Discipline   Date completed: _____

Scripture memory verse selected: _____

6. A Treasured Possession Date completed: _____
7. The Search Is Over   Date completed: _____
8. Abiding in Christ   Date completed: _____
9. It's in God's Hands   Date completed: _____
10. The True Royal Family Date completed: _____

Scripture memory verse selected: _____

11. Return to Your First Love Date completed: _____
12. The Rewards of Love Date completed: _____
13. The Spirit of Love   Date completed: _____
14. Not a Loser   Date completed: _____

15. Loving God, Loving Others   Date completed: _____

    Scripture memory verse selected: _____

16. A True Friend   Date completed: _____
17. Being a Real Friend   Date completed: _____
18. More on Being a Real Friend   Date completed: _____
19. Your Best Friend   Date completed: _____
20. Forgiving Yourself   Date completed: _____

    Scripture memory verse selected: _____

21. The Dating Trap   Date completed: _____
22. The Desires of Your Heart   Date completed: _____
23. Dangerous and Deadly Dating   Date completed: _____
24. Treat Them Right   Date completed: _____
25. Fix Your Eyes   Date completed: _____

    Scripture memory verse selected: _____

26. Built-In Consequences   Date completed: _____
27. Think About the Future   Date completed: _____
28. You Are Not Your Own   Date completed: _____
29. It's Not Just You   Date completed: _____
30. Breaking the Chains   Date completed: _____

    Scripture memory verse selected: _____

31. Second Chance   Date completed: _____
32. Give Your Bod to God   Date completed: _____
33. Rethink How You Think   Date completed: _____
34. First-Frame Thinking   Date completed: _____
35. Choose to Think the Truth   Date completed: _____

Scripture memory verse selected: _____

36. Dead to Sin   Date completed: _____
37. You Have New Life   Date completed: _____
38. Strongholds in the Mind   Date completed: _____
39. Destroying the Devil's Work Date completed: _____
40. Breaking the Strongholds   Date completed: _____

Scripture memory verse selected: _____

Our prayer is that this book would point you to the love, acceptance, freedom and joy that will be yours when you walk with Jesus. We also hope that this book can help open up many ministry opportunities for you to share these truths with others. May God bless your time with Him!

—Neil and Dave

Part One

Ultimate Love

His Love Is Love

We know and rely on the love God has for us. God is love. Whoever lives in love lives in God, and God in him (1 John 4:16).

Now there's a verse you can memorize! And you know what? You really should. When the Bible says God is love, it isn't just saying that God does random acts of kindness. It's saying that God by His very nature is love. He doesn't just *act* lovely, He *is* love.

"Nature" means the necessary parts within something. We could say that the nature of milkshakes is to have ice cream in them. This is true because ice cream is one of the necessary parts. So when we say that God is by His very nature love, we are saying that God not only *contains* love but, like the ice cream in the milkshake, which becomes mixed in with every part of the milkshake, God's love is mixed in with every part of Him.

God never does anything that it isn't an act of love. Have you ever tried to get the ice cream separated from the milkshake once you mixed it in? It doesn't come apart, does it? That's how it is with God and love. His great love is mixed in with everything He does. God, by His very nature, is love.

The Bible says that God never changes: "Jesus Christ is the same yesterday and today and forever" (Hebrews 13:8). So we know that God will always be a loving God.

Have you ever thought, "If God is love, then how come there's so much sin and evil in the world?" Or, "Why did God put us on this awful planet where sin and hate seem to be everywhere?" If we're honest, we have all asked those questions. Did you know the Bible gives us the answers?

When God created the earth He had a special place prepared for Adam and Eve called the Garden of Eden (Genesis 2:15). There was no shame there (Genesis 2:25) because there was no sin! But something terrible happened: Adam and Eve chose to disobey God. In Genesis 2:17 God gave them a single command: "You must not eat from the tree of the knowledge of good and evil." So guess what Adam and Eve decided to do, with a little influence from a snaky friend of theirs? They ate! Genesis 3:6-8 records their sin and their shame and the fall of all mankind.

(If you have some extra time you may want to read Genesis 3:1-15.)

God didn't put us on a planet that was covered with sin and shame. God gave us a great home, but we as mankind chose to disobey God and allow sin and shame to take over. Sin brings death and separation from God (Romans 5:12). But God didn't give up and just let us go to the hell we deserved; He let love take over. Romans 5:8 says, "God demonstrates *his own love* for us in this: While we were still sinners, Christ died for us." The fall of mankind in Eden did more than bring sin into the world. The worst part of it was that sin made it impossible for God to have an intimate, personal relationship with us. God wants to do more than rescue us from sin and death; He wants to lavish us with His love.

I (Dave) have three children—David, Ashley, and Dani. They are older now and out of the diaper stage. But there was a time when all three of them were running around in

Pampers. I travel a great deal, so when I came home my kids treated me like I was a returning war hero. I would come through the front door and they would drop everything and come running toward me.

More than once, however, I would come home and find that something was very wrong. First there was this thick haze hanging over the living room, and a smell like death. My worst fears were confirmed as the three children ran toward me. Two could run with ease, but one of them would wobble like a car with a flat tire. The problem was easy to deduce: One of them had about 20 pounds too much in his or her Pamper. I would yell—

"Stay right there! Don't move!"

"You did the pooh-pooh's, didn't you?"

He or she would look at me with a guilt-riddled face and puppy-dog eyes meant to induce sympathy. Then I would say:

"You did the stinky pooh-pooh!"

"Now get out of here—Go on! Get!"

Would I say that? No way! I did the same thing you're going to do when you're a mom or dad: I invited the pooh-pooh to come.

"Come on! Come here! Come to Daddy!"

Then I would kneel down and get on the same level as my stinky child and actually pick him up. Why? Because I have a pooh-pooh fetish? No! Because there is a baby in there somewhere.

I think you know where I'm going with this! We did the pooh-pooh. We have all sinned. But Jesus was willing to come to earth in the form of a man, actually coming down to our level, picking us up and cleaning us off.

As a dad you know I want to clean up the child, but remember that the child wants to be cleaned up as well.

God demonstrated His great fatherly nature, a love nature, and rescued us from sin and death and cleaned us up. Why? So that we might be able to enjoy an intimate and personal love relationship with Him. John 1:12 tells us "To all who received him, to those who believed in his name, he gave the right to become children of God."

Love Lessons

What does the term "nature" mean as it applies to God's love for us?

When you think of God's love, what comes to mind? Take some time to write out three things you think best demonstrate that God is love to you personally.

How did God demonstrate His love for us when we were sinful?

Why did God go to so much trouble to save us, forgive us of our sins, and clean us up?

The Lie to Reject

I reject the lie that God is unloving, distant, or unfair.

The Truth to Accept

I accept the truth that God is love and that He showed His great love for me when Jesus died for me on the cross.

Prayer for Today

Dear heavenly Father, thank You for loving me so much. I know my sins have been paid for by the precious blood of Jesus Christ and that He has forgiven and accepted me. Help me to understand the great depths of Your love for me. In Jesus' name I pray. Amen.

Today's Bible Reading

Proverbs 1:1-19
Theme: Avoid bad company

The Greatest Act of Love

This is how we know what love is: Jesus Christ laid down his life for us (1 John 3:16).

Love, the truest love, has already been shown to us. It was demonstrated to us through Christ's death on the cross. Almost everyone knows that Christ died, but few stop to think about how awful, yet loving, His death was.

(If you have an extra minute read Matthew 27:32-54.)

Jesus' crucifixion on the cross was about six hours long. The first three hours He suffered at the hands of man, *suffering because of the sinfulness of people like us.* The second three hours His suffering was at the hand of God, *suffering to take away our sinfulness.* Four incredible things happened that day on the cross:

1. Jesus became *sin* for us.
2. He was *separated* from the Father.
3. He paid the total *penalty* for our sin.
4. He made possible a new and abundant *life* in Him.

Christ's suffering was a powerful demonstration of love. If we could take a trip back in time and actually see Christ's death, what would we have seen? The pictures aren't pretty but we need to gaze at them because they show us the depths of Jesus' love for us.

(Take some time and read Isaiah 53.)

Jesus is stripped and bound between two columns. His hands are tied with leather straps to the large brass rings on the columns. He is then beaten by two men, each one alternating blows with their long whips. Their whips are made of leather, and at the end of each strand is either a lead ball or chips of bone and broken pottery. Jesus is whipped over His shoulders and back; even His thighs and calves are beaten.

His skin begins to tear away as the bits of bone sink deep into his flesh. Jesus loses a tremendous amount of blood. His human body becomes weak. He has been up all night, yet He doesn't say a word. He doesn't even open His mouth. Jesus probably slumps to the ground as His executioners give Him the last blows. They only stop because they are told not to kill him. Christ is given a purple soldier's cape, a mocking symbol of His royalty. This stops some of the blood from flowing from His back. He is also given a crown of 2½-inch Judean thorns. They thrust it down on His head. The blood flows down His face into His eyes.

They then began to mock and beat Him, punching Him in the face and tearing out handfuls of His beard. The blood flows, but again Jesus is quiet. They slap Him and spit on Him, mocking Him and calling Him "King of the Jews." Jesus is taken before Pilate, the Roman ruler of Israel. Pilate is swayed by the people to release Barabbas a known murderer, and to crucify Jesus, even though Jesus has broken no laws.

Jesus is given a wooden crossbeam weighing approximately 125 pounds. Barefoot and bound, Jesus now travels some 650 yards up hill to the place of the skull, where common criminals were executed. The Romans wonder if He will die before He reaches the top. Christ's upper back begins to bleed even more as the heavy beam rubs on His shoulders. Christ is so weak now that Simon of Cyrene is finally made to carry the cross the rest of the way to the top of the hill.

Jesus is now at the top. His back is placed on the cross-beam. The executioner takes out a long square metal nail and rips it through the front fold of His hand or wrist. The other hand is nailed with a single blow.

Christ is now lifted some seven feet into the air by His hands to the vertical beam. His knees are bent, His left foot is placed against the rough timber, and another square nail is driven through His foot. Christ's right foot is placed over the left one and a second nail is driven through both feet, locking them together.

His body begins to cramp, every muscle tightening. He thirsts for air. To get it, He has to push on His nailed feet and move up and down on the cross. He moves down to let air in, up to let air out. Jesus goes through this process for the next six hours.

But the worst torment is yet to come. He is now totally separated from the Father. The sky turns to total darkness and the earth begins to shake. Many graves are opened and dead people are resurrected and roaming the city. Jesus cries out, "My God, my God, why have You forsaken me?" Yet all this doesn't kill Jesus; rather, He surrenders His life willingly. Speaking one last time He says, "Into your hands I commit my spirit." Jesus' head slumps forward and He is physically dead.

LOVE LESSON

When you read the account of Christ death, how did it make you feel?

Maybe you have read other accounts of Christ's sacrifice. Did God show you anything new as you read through it this time?

Match the following verses with the correct phrase.
- Romans 6:23; Ephesians 1:7
- John 5:24; John 10:10
- Romans 8:3; 2 Corinthians 5:21
- Matthew 27:46

1. Jesus became *sin* for us.
2. He was *separated* from the Father.
3. He paid the total *penalty* for our sin.
4. He made possible a new and abundant *life* in Him.

The Lie to Reject

I reject the lie that God doesn't love me.

The Truth to Accept

I accept the truth that God showed the great love He has for me through His death on the cross.

Prayer for Today

Dear heavenly Father, I can't even begin to imagine what You went through to pay the penalty for my sin. Your love for me is so awesome. Thank You for Your Son, for His death, and the salvation that He purchased for me. In Jesus' name I pray. Amen.

Today's Bible Reading

Proverbs 1:20-33
Theme: If wisdom could talk

A TOUCH OF HIS LOVE

For God so loved the world that he gave his one and only Son, that whoever believes in him shall not perish but have eternal life. For God did not send his Son into the world to condemn the world, but to save the world through him.

Whoever believes in him is not condemned, but whoever does not believe stands condemned already because he has not believed in the name of God's one and only Son (John 3:16-18).

God's love for us was the ultimate expression of love. How would you define God's ultimate love? Take a moment and write down your thoughts. "Ultimate" is usually defined as final, ending, most extreme.

So how is "extreme" defined? It is defined as greatly exceeding; going far beyond the bounds of moderation; the two ends of the farthest limits of anything. And how does love show itself? Love is an intense care and concern for another person.[1]

God's ultimate love goes far beyond all the known limits of earthly affection. Most of the time we love because someone does something for us. He or she is kind and loving to us so we are kind and loving toward him in return. But God loved us when we couldn't do anything for Him. Jesus told a story about God's great love, and I hope you won't mind if we take the liberty of modernizing it a bit.

(To read original version of the Prodigal Son check out Luke 15:11-32.)

There was a wealthy businessman with two sons who did really well in the stock market and real estate. One of the sons was really straight, respectable, dependable, and all that. But the younger one wasn't very responsible. He would just hang out and surf in the summer and ski in the winter. One day he said to his father, "Dad, give me my share of your estate. After all, I don't want to get your money when you die and I'm so old I can't enjoy it. Give it to me *now* so I can make my own name in life."

So the dad divided his property between the two sons. Not long after that the younger son took his money and went traveling through Europe and foreign lands and spent all his cash on wild living. Nothing was too expensive or out of bounds: whiskey, women, and the whole wild-life thing. He had tons of friends and was the life of the party.

He wasn't a very good bookkeeper, however. In fact, he didn't even know how to balance his checkbook. Soon, without realizing it, he had spent everything. To make matters worse, there was a economic collapse and the whole country went into a recession. He was really hard up for cash, so he filed for unemployment and started to look for a job. Pretty soon the unemployment ran out. He got so desperate that he even filled out an application at McDonald's, but even they wouldn't hire him.

But finally he found work: He was hired to feed the pigs with the other migrant workers. He got so hungry that filling his stomach with the slop that the pigs were eating didn't seem like a bad option. He went back to his party friends, but they wouldn't even talk to him or return his calls. No one would give him anything.

Then one day he woke up. I don't mean he woke up from sleeping, I mean he came to his senses. He said, "How many of my dad's workers have food to spare, and here I am starving to death? I'll go back to my dad and say to him: 'Father, I've blown it! I've sinned against God and against you. I am no longer worthy to be called your son. Please make me one of your hired men.'"

So he got up and went to his father. But while he was still a long way off, his father saw him and was filled with compassion for him. He ran to his son, threw his arms around him, and wouldn't stop hugging him. The son said to him, "Father, I have sinned against God and against you. I am no longer worthy to be called your son." But the father said to his butler, "Quick! Bring the best clothes and put it on him. Put a ring on his finger and good shoes on his feet. Call the caterers and have them bring over the best meal money can buy. Let's have a party and celebrate. For this son of mine was dead and he is alive again. He was lost and is found." So they began to celebrate.

Meanwhile, the older son was busy at the office handling some important accounts when one of the servants e-mailed him to come home. When he came near the house, he heard music and dancing. So he called one of the servants and asked him what was going on. "Your brother has come home," he replied, "and your father is throwing him a big party because he has him back safe and sound."

The older brother became angry and refused to go in. So his father went out and pleaded with him. But he answered his father, "Look! All these years I've been slaving for you and never disobeyed your orders. Yet you never gave me even a small party so I could celebrate with my friends. But when this son of yours, who has spent all your money on prostitutes and drugs comes home, you spare no expense on him!" "My son," the father said, "you are always with me, and everything I have is yours. But we had to celebrate and be glad, because this brother of yours was dead and is alive again; he was lost and is found."

God's love for us isn't based on our performance or even our faithfulness. He loves us because He chooses to. The religious people of Jesus' day were like the good son, but Jesus was saying through His story that God loves everyone and He wants everyone to come back to God the Father. Second Peter 3:9 tells us, "The Lord is not slow in keeping his promise, as some understand slowness. He is patient with you, not wanting anyone to perish, but everyone to come to repentance."

Love Lessons

What did the Prodigal Son do to earn his father's love?

What do we do to earn God's love?

How did the father's love for the son make you feel?

How does God's love for you make you feel?

The Lie to Reject

I reject the lie that I have to perform well to earn God's love and acceptance.

The Truth to Accept

I accept the truth that God loves and accepts me just as I am, but I desire to turn away from my old ways and follow God's ways.

Prayer for Today

Dear heavenly Father, I am so thankful that You love me just as I am and that I don't have to perform to a certain level to receive Your wonderful love, but I do want to live my life for You. I choose to turn from my sinful ways like the Prodigal Son and come back to You. Please show me the things I need to turn from. In Jesus' name I pray. Amen.

Today's Bible Reading

Proverbs 2:1-22
Theme: Avoid wild people

Day Four

He Calls Us Friend

I no longer call you servants, because a servant does not know his master's business. Instead, I have called you friends, for everything that I learned from my Father I have made known to you (John 15:15).

It seems strange that we often know that God loves us but fail to realize that He also wants to be our friend. He is not just available for an ordinary friendship but is actually open to the idea of becoming our very best friend. Jesus wants to be our companion and guide throughout all our lives and even in eternity. He wants us to share all our business with Him and what's even more exciting is that the God of the universe wants to share His business with us.

Think about what He's up to! Just look at some of the simple stuff. God is busy with the whole universe. Scientists and scholars have concluded that the Master Planner left nothing to chance.

The slant of the earth, for example, tilted at an angle of 23 degrees, produces our seasons. Scientists tell us that if the earth had not been tilted exactly as it is, vapors from the oceans would move both north and south, piling up continents of ice.

If the moon were only 50,000 miles away from earth instead of 200,000 miles the tides might be so enormous that all continents would be submerged in water—even the mountains would be eroded.

If the crust of the earth had been only ten feet thicker, there would be no oxygen and without it all animal life would die.

Had the oceans been a few feet deeper, carbon dioxide and oxygen would have been absorbed and no plant life would exist.[2]

God is busy with a lot of stuff. You might think that, like some earthly dads, God may not have time for you or that there must be other more important saints to talk to and befriend.

Nothing could be further from the truth. Because He's God, He never gets too busy, nor is He a respecter of persons. He's willing to be friends with anyone who will put his or her faith and trust in Christ and begin a friendship through His Son.

Friends may bail on you, but God never will. Growing up in Montana, I (Dave) heard a lot of bear stories, and some of them might even be true. One of the more popular stories goes something like this.

Two men were backpacking through Glacier National Park. Glacier is one of the few places in the U.S. where you can still come across a wild grizzly bear. The most dangerous is a mother bear with cubs. As the two men headed down the trail they heard branches breaking about a hundred yards in front of them. It was an old sow grizzly with two cubs. Both men froze, hoping desperately that she would not see them or smell them. Sadly, the wind blew their scent right at her. The two men began to hightail it out of there when suddenly one of the men sat down on the ground and began to take off his backpack and hiking boots.

"What in the world are you doing?" shouted the other man.

By this time the first hiker had replaced his heavy hiking boots with his light running shoes.

"Well," he exclaimed confidently, "it occurred to me that I don't need to outrun the bear—I only need to outrun you!"[3]

Some friend he turned out to be! Have you ever been deserted by a friend? Left behind? Jesus is a friend who sticks closer to you than a brother. And He promises that He will never leave you or forsake you (Matthew 28:20).

Jesus went to great lengths to show His love for people and how much He desired intimate and personal friendships with us. Read the Gospel account of the little man Zacchaeus. Would Jesus ever want to start a friendship with a tax collector, a man who was given a license from the Roman government to steal from his own people? Zacchaeus was hated by almost everyone, yet Jesus initiated a friendship with him.

> Jesus entered Jericho and was passing through. A man was there by the name of Zacchaeus; he was a chief tax collector and was wealthy. He wanted to see who Jesus was, but being a short man he could not, because of the crowd. So he ran ahead and climbed a sycamore-fig tree to see him, since Jesus was coming that way. When Jesus reached the spot, he looked up and said to him, "Zacchaeus, come down immediately. I must stay at your house today." So he came down at once and welcomed him gladly. All the people saw this and began to mutter, "He has gone to be the guest of a 'sinner.'" But Zacchaeus stood up and said to the Lord, "Look, Lord! Here and now I give half of my possessions to the poor, and if I have cheated anybody out of anything, I will pay back four times the amount." Jesus said to him, "Today salvation has come to this house, because this

man, too, is a son of Abraham. For the Son of Man came to seek and to save what was lost" (Luke 19:1-9).

When Jesus said, "I must stay at your house today," at first glance and from our cultural background it sounds like Jesus just rudely invited Himself to dinner. In Jesus' day, however, your home was a place for close family and friends to fellowship, not a place for strangers. What Jesus was really saying is that He wanted to start a permanent friendship with Zacchaeus. He wanted to fellowship with him.

Did you know that Jesus gives us the same offer? Revelation 3:20 quotes Jesus saying, "Here I am! I stand at the door and knock. If anyone hears my voice and opens the door, I will come in and eat with him, and he with me." Jesus isn't looking for a free lunch. He wants to fellowship with you and become your best friend.

Jesus doesn't care about your reputation—just look at Zacchaeus. He was a chief tax collector and a known sinner. When Jesus said he would go to his house, "all the people saw this and began to mutter, 'He has gone to be the guest of a sinner.'" Jesus knows our background and where we are coming from. All of us have sinned (Romans 3:23). He didn't come to call the righteous but to seek and save those who are lost. Only through a personal and intimate relationship with Jesus can we get radically right with God (Romans 10:9,10). But accepting Jesus as your Savior does more than provide you with a ticket to heaven; it opens the door to a deeply intimate and personal friendship with God.

Love Lessons

Have you ever felt like God was distant and unfriendly? If so, describe how you felt at that time.

How would you describe an intimate friendship with God? What would it look like?

How have Zacchaeus' story (Luke 19), Revelation 3:20, and John 15:15 shaped your view of God and a friendship with Him?

THE LIE TO REJECT

I reject the lie that God would never want to be friends with me.

THE TRUTH TO ACCEPT

I accept the truth that God desires a close and intimate friendship with me.

PRAYER FOR TODAY

Dear heavenly Father, I thank You so much that You are not only my great and awesome God but You are also my friend. I choose to not keep You locked outside of any room in my life. I gladly open the door of my life to You and ask You to fellowship with me. I desire that You would be my best friend and guide in life. In Jesus' name I pray. Amen.

TODAY'S BIBLE READING

Proverbs 3:1-12
Theme: Trusting God

LOVING DISCIPLINE

The Lord disciplines those he loves, and he punishes everyone he accepts as a son (Hebrews 12:6).

Discipline: Just the sound of it can make your stomach turn. I (Dave) can remember being disciplined by my parents, my older sisters, my schoolteachers, my principals, my neighbors . . . anyway, you get the point. Some of those people disciplined out of love and some of them didn't.

What comes to mind when you think of discipline? Do you think of the Marine sergeant who shouts out, "You did it now, you slimy, good-for-nothing maggot! How could you be so stupid? Well, now you're going to have to pay! Drop to the floor and give me a hundred one-armed push-ups and stop crying, you big baby!" Or do you picture a calm and patient father who loves so deeply that his eyes are filled with tears because he hurts knowing he has to discipline you? Sadly, some of us have experienced something closer to the first scene.

When God says He disciplines us because He loves us, what does He mean? Well, Hebrews 12:6-10 gives us some good insights.

> The Lord disciplines those he loves, and he punishes everyone he accepts as a son. Endure hardship as discipline; God is treating you as sons. For what son is not disciplined by his father? If you are not disciplined (and everyone undergoes discipline), then you are illegiti-

mate children and not true sons. Moreover, we have all had human fathers who disciplined us and we respected them for it. How much more should we submit to the Father of our spirits and live!

Our fathers disciplined us for a little while as they thought best; but God disciplines us for our good, that we may share in his holiness.

God is love, so everything He does is done in love. Even when God is angry at sin, it is a loving anger. When He pours out His wrath, it's a loving wrath. We don't usually think about wrath and anger as being connected to love, because we usually don't see the whole picture and what God is going to accomplish with His loving discipline.

I saw something when I was traveling through Europe that I think will help you better understand God's loving discipline. As I traveled through Italy, I made a point to see the works of the great artist Michelangelo. He is one of my favorite sculptors and painters. (I think I like him so much because when he painted and sculpted Jesus, he showed Him as a strong and masculine Savior. I never have liked the depictions of Jesus as a thin, helpless-looking man.) While in Italy I went to the world-famous Academy. This museum houses several of Michelangelo's works including some unfinished ones.

As I examined the sculptures from a distance they look smooth and lifelike. But as I looked closer at the stone I could see that the surface was covered with tiny little marks from Michelangelo's chisel. He must have hammered at each piece of marble thousands of time to break away the unwanted stone—never hitting the sculpture too hard or it might break, but hammering just enough to shape a beautiful masterpiece.

To me that's a picture of God's loving discipline. God is removing the unwanted parts of our flawed character and smoothing out our rough edges so that we will one day resemble Jesus. Hebrews tells us that if this process isn't going on in our lives it's a good reason to question whether we're truly born again: "God is treating you as sons. For what son is not disciplined by his father? If you are not disciplined (and everyone undergoes discipline), then you are illegitimate children and not true sons." God's love is at work in discipline.

Picture for a moment a star athlete like Dave Johnson. You might remember him from the Reebok commercials: Who is the world's greatest athlete, Dan or Dave? Or maybe you remember Dave because he won the bronze metal in the Barcelona Olympics in 1992 even though he had a severe injury. Dave is probably America's best decathlete. He is in constant training because, as a decathlete, Dave goes through ten grueling events. They are the 100-meter dash, long jump, shotput, high jump, 400 meters, 110-meter hurdles, discus, pole vault, javelin, and 1500-meter run. Just writing them out exhausted me!

What if Dave was never disciplined by his coaches or had no self discipline? "All right, Dave, today I want you to run the 1500-meter race, but before you do I brought you a few snacks. Here's some deep dish pizza, and feel free to down this liter of Dr. Pepper and eat three or four of these Twinkies—and don't forget the chips and salsa I brought you. They're great!" What would happen to Dave if he ate all that junk food and then ran the 1500-meter race? He'd be puking his guts out after just a few laps. Dave would never train that way because he has his eye on the prize, the final goal, and he sees discipline as his friend.

Paul gives in a similar illustration 1 Corinthians 9:24-27. He writes, "Do you not know that in a race all the runners run, but only one gets the prize? Run in such a way as to get the prize. Everyone who competes in the games goes into strict training. They do it to get a crown that will not last; but we do it to get a crown that will last forever. Therefore I do not run like a man running aimlessly; I do not fight like a man beating the air. No, I beat my body and make it my slave so that after I have preached to others, I myself will not be disqualified for the prize." Also in Philippians 3:14 Paul states, "I press on toward the goal to win the prize for which God has called me heavenward in Christ Jesus."

Do you see God's discipline as a friend? Do you understand that God is training you to run a good race and is teaching you how to be more like Jesus?

LOVE LESSONS

Why does the Lord discipline those He loves? How can discipline be love?

Why do we respect fathers who discipline us in love?

If there is no discipline in our life from God, what is that a sign of?

THE LIE TO REJECT

I reject the lie that God's discipline is mean, evil, or unloving.

THE TRUTH TO ACCEPT

I accept the truth that God disciplines out of love and that He is always doing what is best for me.

PRAYER FOR TODAY

Dear heavenly Father, I thank You so much that You discipline me. I know that You love me and that You are conforming me to the image of Christ. I, like Paul, want to press on toward the goal to win the prize for which You have called me. I want to be like Jesus. Help me to see Your discipline as a friend and not compare it to the bad, earthly examples I have in my life. I know You are love, so I know I can trust You to guide and care for me. Amen.

TODAY'S BIBLE READING

Proverbs 3:13-20
Theme: Wisdom's worth

Part Two

God's Chosen Ones

DAY SIX

A TREASURED POSSESSION

You are a people holy to the LORD your God. The LORD your God has chosen you out of all the peoples on the face of the earth to be his people, his treasured possession. The LORD did not set his affection on you and choose you because you were more numerous than other peoples, for you were the fewest of all peoples. But it was because the LORD loved you and kept the oath he swore to your forefathers that he brought you out with a mighty hand and redeemed you from the land of slavery, from the power of Pharaoh king of Egypt. Know therefore that the LORD your God is God; he is the faithful God, keeping his covenant of love to a thousand generations of those who love him and keep his commands (Deuteronomy 7:6-9).

Everyone likes to be chosen. Even if it's just a game of touch football on a Sunday afternoon with the church youth group, we all like to be picked. Have you ever asked yourself the question "Why did God pick me?" Of all the people in the whole world, how come God picked *me*? In addition, God doesn't just *like* you, He actually *loves* you. You're a *treasured possession* to Him. Anyone who calls on the name of the Lord can be saved and become part of the family of God (Romans 10:13). When we accept Christ, our relationship with God is restored and we are made holy by the blood of Christ.

Take some time right now and think about God's love for you and why He has chosen you to be His child.

God doesn't pick people for the same reasons we pick people. We usually pick those who can help us. Like with that football team, we look around at all our choices and pick the fastest runners, or the person who would make the best quarterback. But God didn't do that. He looked around and found the nation of Israel. Did God pick them because they were the biggest and strongest, because they had the best economy and were the most committed to Him? No!

> The Lord did not set his affection on you and choose you because you were more numerous than other peoples, for you were the fewest of all peoples.

God picked Israel because He wanted to! God doesn't need any help. He doesn't have to pick the best players to win. God made a promise to a guy named Abraham a long time ago, that He would start a new nation. He also promised that from this group of people would come the Messiah, Jesus. Well, we can look back at this passage in Deuteronomy and see that God keeps His promises.

> Know therefore that the Lord your God is God; he is the faithful God, keeping his covenant of love to a thousand generations of those who love him and keep his commands.

A covenant is a promise. God's promise was to love for a thousand generations, and even though God's people have not always been faithful in following Him, God still kept His promise and sent the Messiah to save us from our sins. That's love! When God makes a promise, He keeps it.

God made another promise to those who have trusted Christ as their Savior.

> Being confident of this, that he who began a good work in you will carry it on to completion until the day of Christ Jesus (Philippians 1:6).

God has begun a good work in you and He is going to accomplish that work of transforming you to the image of Christ. No matter what God has to work with, He can transform it to the image of Christ! Have you ever felt like God made a mistake because He made you a certain way? And that if He had just made you in a different way then you could live for Him and be the Christian that He has called you to be? I think everyone has had that thought a time or two!

When I (Dave) was younger, about six years old I used to stutter. I used to say, "Here come Gram-m-ma and Gramm-m-ma"; I never could say "Grandpa." The poor guy probably had a complex—his own grandson couldn't even say his name! I am also mildly dyslexic, which means my mind flips the letters of the alphabet around so I can't read them very easily. (Don't ever try to pick up my personal phone list. I don't know who you'll call. When I look at it, however, it all makes sense to me.)

To top it all off, I never learned how to read until I was halfway through the fourth grade. Could God ever use an illiterate, dyslexic, stutterer to become a speaker and a writer? Well, that's what He's doing in my life. I think God loves to take things that are broken and use them, just so no one makes the mistake of thinking that it was the person's greatness that produced this good fruit!

If God is at work, look out, because there isn't anything He can't do. You may think, "Wow, what a miracle God has done in your life, Dave!" It's true—it is a miracle, but God is doing a miraculous work in all of us by conforming us to the image of Christ. Romans 8:29 says, "Those God foreknew he also predestined to be conformed to the likeness of his Son, that he might be the firstborn among many brothers."

Love Lessons

What does it mean to be conformed to the likeness of Jesus?

How have you seen God conforming you to the likeness of Christ?

What areas do you think God still needs to work on in your life?

The Lie to Reject

I renounce the lie that I don't belong to God.

The Truth to Accept

I accept the truth that God has chosen me and that I am part of the family of God.

Prayer for Today

Dear heavenly Father, I thank You for choosing me. I know, Lord, that You have chosen me, just one of all the peoples on the face of the earth to be one of Your children, one of Your treasured possessions. Lord, I know You didn't choose me because I was better than anyone else, Lord, You are God and You are a faithful God, who keeps His promise of love to a thousand generations of those who love You and keep Your commands. Lord, I want to keep Your commandments and live for You. In Jesus' name I pray. Amen.

Today's Bible Reading

Proverbs 3:21-35
Theme: Kindness and gentleness

Day Seven

The Search Is Over

You are the body of Christ, and each one of you is a part of it (1 Corinthians 12:27).

Most students we talk to don't naturally feel good about themselves. The natural man (every person who hasn't trusted Christ) has no identity in Christ, so from the time we are born into this world we search for some sense of identity, purpose, and meaning in life. Fortunately, we don't have to search very hard to find our identity. In fact, we have a God who searches for us and gives us a new identity through our relationship with Him.

It's like the owner who lost his dog and placed this ad in the lost-and-found section of the newspaper:

> **LOST DOG**—$50 reward, black-and-tan dog of poodle and German shepherd descent. Flea-bitten, right hind leg missing, no hair on rump, blind, and recently neutered. Answers to the name **"Lucky."**

After reading about that dog you may think he has had a terrible life. He isn't lucky! But you know he really is because he has a master that cares enough for him to try to find him even though he isn't much to look at and is in such bad shape.[1]

More and more, people are searching for some sense of significance, and are attempting to find it within themselves. That thinking has even found its way into the church.

So the question is, "Where *does* a person find a legitimate sense of identity or worth?" Is it in talents? No, it can't possibly be. God has given some people one talent, some two talents, and others five talents (see Matthew 25:14-28). You may say, "Well, God, how could You do that? Don't You know that the only person who can have any legitimate sense of worth or identity is the five-talented person?" But that is not true. We know a lot of five-talented people who are struggling for a sense of worth just like the one-talented person.

Well, then, does our worth lie in intelligence? No, because according to 1 Corinthians 1:27, "God chose the foolish things of the world to shame the wise." Okay, how about appearance? If we only appeared good, certainly we would have the acceptance and affirmation of others. But according to Isaiah 53:2, Jesus had "no beauty or majesty to attract us to him."

That dog may not look good to us or have any worth to you or me but he has worth to his master. Why? Because the master loves him!

Is our worth found in spiritual gifts? No, I'm sure it is not. God has not equally distributed gifts, talents or intelligence, but He has equally distributed *Himself*. Our identity comes from *knowing who we are as children of God*, and our sense of worth grows out of our commitment to become like Him.

Show me people today who know who they are as children of God and have committed themselves to Him, and I'll show you those who have a profound sense of self and of worth. Show me somebody who is continually growing in the fruit of the Spirit, whose life is characterized by love, joy, peace, patience, goodness, faithfulness, gentleness, and self-control. Will that person have a good sense of identity and value? Yes, I'm sure of it. And the beautiful part of this truth is that everyone has exactly the same opportunity.

God has placed an ad in the lost and found section for everyone to see.

> **LOST:** all mankind—people of mixed ancestry. Spotted with sin, spiritually blind, hard-hearted, and riddled with pride. Tend to go their own way. Reward to any who calls on the name "Jesus."

Jesus gives us more than eternal life when we call upon Him. He gives us *membership into His family* and a *new identity*.

Some people appear to play such a big part as a member of Christ's body, while others may feel they are not needed. But Paul writes in 1 Corinthians 12:21,22, "The eye cannot say to the hand, 'I don't need you!' And the head cannot say to the feet, 'I don't need you!' On the contrary, those parts of the body that seem to be weaker are indispensable, and the parts that we think are less honorable we treat with special honor." I'm glad God gives special honors, because we have a tendency to ignore those who are less gifted or talented. Our pursuit in life must be to fully utilize the gifts we have.

When I (Neil) first entered ministry and before I understood these truths myself, a young lady came to our church college department. She was not very attractive and seemed to be untalented. Her heritage was horrible: Her father was a drunken bum who had left his family several years earlier; her older brother ran drugs in and out of the house, causing nothing but problems; her mother eked out a living working at two mediocre jobs.

This young lady knew she could not compete with the world's system, but what she could and did do was to find out who she was as a child of God. I have never seen a girl who had a healthier sense of identity and worth. She became the friend of everybody, and she ended up with the nicest guy in our youth department.

In those days I used to wonder, *What is this girl's secret? What does she have?* Well, she understood at that time, more than I did, what it meant to be a child of God and to commit herself to being all He wanted her to be. She took on that identity, followed it faithfully, and enjoyed her Christianity much more than most people do.

LOVE LESSONS

What are some of the things you have seen your friends or people you know base their identity on?

Where does our identity in Christ come from?

What does new life in Christ bring you?

THE LIE TO REJECT

I renounce the lie that I can find worth in anything except my relationship to Christ.

THE TRUTH TO ACCEPT

I accept the truth that God has given me a new identity in Christ and that I'm part of His body, the church.

Prayer for Today

Dear heavenly Father, I thank You for making me a member of Your Body. I renounce the lie that I have no part to play or no significant contribution to make in the body of Christ. I accept what You have created in me and the special spiritual gifts that come from You. I commit myself to grow in Your likeness so that my gifts and abilities can be used to edify Your church.

I renounce the lie that my identity and sense of worth is found in my ability to perform. I accept the truth that my identity and worth is found in Christ and will be realized increasingly as I grow in Christ's likeness. I thank You for allowing me to be a part of Your family. I realize that I not only have You as my Father, but I have brothers and sisters in Christ with whom I can share my life. In the wonderful name of Jesus I pray. Amen.

Today's Bible Reading

Proverbs 4:1-9
Theme: Get wisdom

Day Eight

Abiding in Christ

You did not choose me, but I chose you and appointed you to go and bear fruit—fruit that will last. Then the Father will give you whatever you ask in my name. This is my command: Love each other (John 15:16,17).

I love the fifteenth chapter of John. It tells us the source of our life and strength, why we are here, and how to bear fruit, and it gives us the goal for our ministry. Jesus is our life, and apart from Him we can do nothing. Many people are waiting for God to choose them or appoint them to some ministry, not realizing that they have already been called and appointed.

We have been called by God to be His children. We are all called and appointed to serve God full-time. Being the mother, father, spouse, carpenter, engineer, homemaker, secretary, lawyer, or politician that God has called us to be is full-time service. I don't think God is overly concerned about whether His children are carpenters, plumbers or engineers. But He does care *what kind* of carpenter, plumber, or engineer we may be. We don't need any pastoral position to serve the Lord, although some people have been called to those positions. The only person who can keep us from being what God wants us to be is ourselves.

Why are we here? To glorify God! How? "This is to my Father's glory, that you bear much fruit, showing yourselves to be my disciples" (John 15:8). Some think that John 15 says we *must* bear fruit. This can lead to tremendous guilt and orient our ministry in the wrong direction.

John 15 is really about abiding in Christ. We aren't required to bear fruit; we are required to *abide in Christ*. The *result* of abiding in Christ is bearing fruit, and that is the proof of our discipleship.

We have been called to bear fruit that remains. Do you consider everything that happened in your life and ministry last year to be a result of your hard work and human ingenuity? If so, then where was God, and how was He glorified by your self-effort? Remember, Jesus intends to pass by the self-sufficient. We can't measure our effectiveness in ministry by our activities; we must evaluate it on the basis of fruit that remains. I want nothing more than to have people say, "You can't account for that man or his ministry apart from God's working through him." Then, and only then, will our joy be made full (see John 15:11) and our heavenly Father be glorified.

The error on the other extreme is to think that abiding in Christ is to sit around in some holy piety. Not so! "If you keep My commandments, you will abide in My love" (John 15:10 NASB). What are His commandments? "This is His commandment, that we believe in the name of His Son, Jesus Christ, and love one another, just as He commanded us. And the one who keeps His commandments abides in Him, and He in him. And we know by this that He abides in us, by the Spirit whom He has given us" (1 John 3:23,24 NASB).

Belief always precedes behavior. The commandment is to *believe* in the name of Jesus Christ. We are to do what we believe and become what we already are in Christ. It is the Holy Spirit who bears witness with our spirit that we are children of God (see Romans 8:16). And it is the Holy Spirit who enables us to walk by faith.

Another motivation for abiding in God is the hope for answered prayer. "If you abide in Me, and My words abide in you, ask whatever you wish, and it shall be done for you.... That your fruit should remain, that whatever you ask of the Father in My name, He may give to you" (John 15:7,16 NASB). When we choose to abide in Christ we are seeking to do His will, which we understand to be good, acceptable and perfect (see Romans 12:2). "Delight yourself in the Lord and he will give you the desires of your heart" (Psalm 37:4). If we abide in Christ, our wishes will be God's wishes, and our desires will be God's desires. But we must first conform to His image. Then our desires and wishes will be in line with His, and whatever we ask will be granted because our desire is to do His will.

If we abide in Christ, what will be the result? We will love one another. The concept of *agape* (love) seems indefinable to many people. But is easy to understand if you realize that the word can be used as either a noun or a verb. When *agape* is used as a noun, it refers to the highest of Christian character:"God is love" (1 John 4:8); "Love is patient, love is kind" (1 Corinthians 13:4). According to 1 Timothy 1:5, "The goal of this command is love, which comes from a pure heart and a good conscience and a sincere faith."

Agape love is not dependent upon the object of love. God loves us because it is His nature to love us, not because we are lovable. If it were any other way, it would be conditional love. So when someone says he cannot love another person, he may be revealing more about his own character than about the other person.

Agape love is also used as a verb in the Bible. Then *agape* becomes an action word, something I would do on your behalf if I loved you. "For God so loved the world that he *gave*" (John 3:16). The application of that verse for our lives is 1 John 3:16,17: "This is how we know what love is: Jesus Christ laid down his life for us. And we ought to lay down our lives for our brothers. If anyone has material possessions and sees his brother in need but has no pity on him, how can the love of God be in him?"

This is not love and action based on feeling. We can't order our feelings toward anyone. But by the grace of God we can do what is right for the other person. We can love the unlovely and show mercy on the poor and suffering.

When I (Neil) was a pastor, I used to greet people after church. One Sunday a dear man in his seventies handed me a note that said, "Pastor, I have learned over the years that one of life's most enduring values is that no one can sincerely help another without helping himself in the process. It is more blessed to give than to receive." As 1 John 4:7 says, "Dear friends, let us love one another, for love comes from God. Everyone who loves has been born of God and knows God."

LOVE LESSONS

Take a minute and ask yourself: "Is the fruit of the Spirit more evident in my life this year than last year?"

"Am I more loving, patient, kind, and self-controlled now than I was a year ago?"

"Did I do something that will have lasting consequences?"

THE LIE TO REJECT

I renounce the lie of Satan that I can produce fruit without God.

THE TRUTH TO ACCEPT

I accept the truth that I can only find my true significance in my relationship to God.

PRAYER FOR TODAY

Dear heavenly Father, I confess that I have tried to bear fruit without You. I have not always accepted my position in life, and have looked for, and waited for, a calling from You, not realizing that You have already called and appointed me to bear fruit right where I am. I have petitioned You without first being submissive. I have not loved people as You have loved them. I renounce the lies of Satan that I can produce fruit without You if I just tried harder on my own.

I don't want to be self-sufficient. I choose to find my significance in my relationship to You. Because my sufficiency is in You, I will trust You to use me to bear fruit that lasts. I want to love like You do. I have no greater desire than to abide in Christ. I now commit myself to a life of faith, believing in You, and by the power of the indwelling Holy Spirit I commit myself to be obedient to Your will. In Jesus' precious name I pray. Amen.

TODAY'S BIBLE READING

Proverbs 4:10-19
Theme: Avoid bad company

IT'S IN GOD'S HANDS

If God is for us, who can be against us? He who did not spare his own Son, but gave him up for us all—how will he not also, along with him, graciously give us all things? Who will bring any charge against those whom God has chosen? It is God who justifies. Who is he that condemns? Christ Jesus, who died—more than that, who was raised to life—is at the right hand of God and is also interceding for us (Romans 8:31-34).

This awesome passage is really dealing with the fact that if God is for us, then no other opposition matters. If God isn't out to get us, then who is? The answer is Satan. Revelation 12:10 says that he accuses the brethren day and night. This relentless enemy of our soul blinds the unbelieving so they cannot see the light of the gospel of the glory of Christ (see 2 Corinthians 4:4). An emissary of Satan is assigned to keep us under the penalty of sin. When you accepted Christ he lost that battle for your life, thanks to Jesus, but he didn't pull in his fangs and curl up his tail. Now he is committed to keeping you under the power of sin, and his chief means of doing that is through deception.

This father of lies (see John 8:44) raises up thoughts against the knowledge of God (see 2 Corinthians 10:5), seeking to distort the nature of our relationship with Him and accusing us day and night. Paul warns us not to be ignorant of Satan's schemes (see 2 Corinthians 2:11), but Christians often operate like blindfolded warriors. Not knowing who our enemy is, we strike out at ourselves and each other.

Satan can't do anything about our position in Christ. However, if he can get us to *believe* our position isn't true, we will live as though it is not. When we surveyed 1725 professing Christian young people, we found that three out of four believe they are different from other kids, that Christianity works for others, but not for them. Is that true? Of course not, but if they believe they are different, will it affect the way they live their lives? Of course it will. Of the same group, seven out of ten said they sometimes heard voices like a subconscious self talking to them.

Now do I believe that seven out of ten Christians we meet are out of their minds? No, I do not believe that! What I believe is 1 Timothy 4:1: "The Spirit clearly says that in later times some will abandon the faith and follow deceiving spirits and things taught by demons." That's happening all over the world today. No matter where I go, that battle is being waged in the minds of people.

Satan's big plan is to destroy our concept of God: to distort the relationship we have with Him, or to discredit the truth of who we really are as children of God. Satan's lies are aimed at causing me to think, *I'm stupid, I'm no good, I'm ugly, God doesn't love me, I can't be forgiven, Christianity doesn't work for me.*

We see this all the time as we lead students through the Steps to Freedom. For example, when we learn that a woman has had sex before marriage and an abortion, we encourage her to assume responsibility for the abortion and to resolve the issue with the following prayer:

"Lord, I confess that I have used my body as an instrument of unrighteousness and conceived a child. I did not assume stewardship of that life, and I ask Your forgiveness. I give that child to You for Your care in eternity. Amen."

One time I (Neil) asked the person to also pray: "And I accept Your forgiveness, Lord, by choosing to accept Your forgiveness of myself." She immediately began experiencing interference, revealing how Satan was holding her in bondage. She believed she could not be forgiven for such a terrible act. Is that true? No, it's a lie. Those accusing, condemning thoughts cannot be from God because He is the One who justifies: "God demonstrates his own love for us in this: While we were still sinners, Christ died for us" (Romans 5:8).

Zechariah 3:1,2 says, "Then he showed me Joshua the high priest standing before the angel of the Lord, and Satan standing at his right side to accuse him. The Lord said to Satan, 'The Lord rebuke you, Satan! The Lord, who has chosen Jerusalem, rebuke you! Is not this man a burning stick snatched from the fire?'"

Joshua was standing before God as the high priest representing the nation of Israel. He was clothed in filthy garments, which was not a good thing. In the Old Testament, when the high priest came before God in the holy of holies on the Day of Atonement, he went through elaborate ceremonial washings so he would not appear defiled before God. The picture we have before us is of a man representing the sins of the people of Israel, and Satan is standing alongside to accuse him. But who does God rebuke? He rebukes *Satan*, proclaiming, "Is not this man a burning stick snatched from the fire?" (Zechariah 3:2). Are we not children of God, snatched from the flames of hell?

What do you suppose God is doing today in the face of Satan's accusations against the children of God? Let me create a scene in the courts of heaven. Who is the Judge? It is God the Father. Who are the accused? You and I. Who is the prosecuting attorney? Satan. Who is the defense attorney? Jesus Christ. Can we lose this court case? There is *no way* we could, because "he is able to save completely those who come to God through him, because he always lives to intercede for them" (Hebrew 7:25).

Jesus is standing at the right hand of the Father, saying, "Look at my side that was pierced. Look at my hands and feet. My sacrifice is sufficient. I died once for all."

What power does Satan have? Can he determine the verdict? Can he pronounce the sentence? No, all he can do is bring forth charges and accusations.

Love Lessons

What is Satan's biggest plan in the battle for our mind?

What does Satan usually accuse you of? How do his accusations make you feel?

What power does Satan really have? Can he pronounce a judgment against us? Why or why not?

The Lie to Reject

I reject the lie that a condemning charge can be pronounced against me.

The Truth to Accept

I accept the truth that since I have accepted Christ as my Savior I am free from any condemning charges that Satan may try to bring against me.

Prayer for Today

Dear heavenly Father, since You are for me, who can be against me? Thank You, Lord, that Your Word tells me that Jesus interceded for me and has freed me from any condemning charges that Satan may bring against me. In Jesus' name. Amen.

Today's Bible Reading

Proverbs 4:20-27
Theme: Watch your step

Day Ten

The True Royal Family

You are a chosen people, a royal priesthood, a holy nation, a people belonging to God, that you may declare the praises of him who called you out of darkness into his wonderful light (1 Peter 2:9).

Every time you turn on the TV you hear something about the royal family: Prince Charles and Lady Diana. I've heard some people say, "Boy, I wish I were royalty— then I'd have all the power and privileges of a king." I suppose it would be nice to be an earthly king, but to be honest with you, I wouldn't trade the position I have in the kingdom of God for anything this world has to offer.

Just look at Lady Di for a second. Now I don't know her personally; all I know is what the newspapers and news shows say, and that should be taken with a grain of salt. But it doesn't take a psychiatrist to figure out that the woman isn't happy. She struggles with depression and bulimia and her marriage ended in tragedy. You see, you can be an earthly king or queen with banks full of money and enough power to influence the whole world, but what good is all of that if you have no peace?

First Peter 2:9 reminds us that we as Christians also have an important possession. We are called *chosen people*. Chosen means we are handpicked by God to be His special treasures. We are so very special to Him because we are blood-related. How are we blood-related, you might ask. Through the shedding of Christ's blood we are allowed to become the children of God.

In addition, this Scripture says we are a *royal priesthood*. If you were part of the royal family in England you would have access to the queen. To be part of God's royal family means you have direct access to God. A priest in the Old Testament was to bring God's Word to the people. But now all of us who are Christians are called priests. Not just some special group in the church but everyone who has accepted Christ is to perform the work of a priest. We are to bring God's Word to the people all around us.

But it doesn't stop there; God declares us to be a *holy nation*. When God uses the term "nation" he means the body of Christ, the church. God has declared the church to be holy. When you put your trust in Christ, you were declared holy, too. To be holy means to be made clean and set apart for God.

Finally, God tops it all off by saying that we belong to Him. We don't run our own life. At first that may seem kind of bad—after all, I want my freedom. But remember that God is a loving and merciful God who is always leading us into what is best for us. The problem we have with our freedom is that we don't even know what is best for us. Because we belong to God He is going to take very good care of us. It's like my children: They tend to take better care of a toy that belongs to them. But we belong to *God*, and we are not just play toys to Him. He calls us by His name.

As you let that passage sink in you begin to realize that we have been given a great position. But with that position come some big responsibilities. We have been called to declare the praises of God. We are to tell how has God brought us out of darkness (sin) and into His wonderful light (holiness). When you see someone living in sin do you put him down or tell him about the God who saved you from the dark powers of sin? I doubt that I'll ever get to meet Prince Charles or Princess Di, but if I do, I know what I'll share with them!

Love Lessons

Are you living like a child of the King, one who has been chosen to be part of God's family, or like common earthly royalty? Does your life have peace?

Have you been fulfilling your role as a priest, telling others about Jesus?

How do you feel when you read that you are God's special treasure? How does this help motivate you to live a holy life and share Christ with others?

The Lie to Reject

I reject the lie that I'm on the outside and don't belong to God and His family.

The Truth to Accept

I accept the truth that I belong to God and that He chose me to be part of His family and that I have been given a special role as a royal priest and part of a holy nation.

Prayer for Today

Dear heavenly Father, thank You that You called me out of darkness and into Your awesome light. I want to tell everyone about You and how You saved me. Help me not to be afraid of what others think about me. I choose to remember what You have said about me—that You call me a royal priest and a holy nation, and that I belong to You. In Jesus' name I pray. Amen.

Today's Bible Reading

Proverbs 5:1-23
Theme: Leave lust in the dust

PART THREE

Loving God

Part Three

Loving God

RETURN TO YOUR FIRST LOVE

Jesus replied: "Love the Lord your God with all your heart and with all your soul and with all your mind." This is the first and greatest commandment (Matthew 22:37,38).

We know that God desires a love relationship with us. He spared no expense to make our relationship with Him possible. He even allowed His Son, Jesus, to die that terrible death on the cross just so we could be forgiven of our sins and know God personally. More than knowing God, however, God wants us to love Him, worship Him, and adore Him.

What if you feel like you don't love God? When you worship God, do you feel like you're just going through the motions? Do things seem different from when you first accepted Christ? If they are, you may have lost your first love. God's Word talks about that in Revelation 2:4,5. Jesus was speaking to the church in Ephesus. They had lost their first love for God.

Here is what Jesus had to say: "Yet I hold this against you: You have forsaken your first love. Remember the height from which you have fallen! Repent and do the things you did at first. If you do not repent, I will come to you and remove your lampstand from its place." "Remove the lamp-stand" means that Jesus would actually stop blessing and empowering the church in Ephesus if they didn't start loving God with their first love. That sounds serious, and it is. If loving God is the greatest commandment then not loving God must be one of the greatest offenses. What can you do if you feel like you have lost your first love?

1. *Remember your first love.* Do you remember how it was when you first accepted Christ as your Savior, how much you loved God when you realized that He gave His Son for you? Part of getting your first love back is to recall those important events. After you recall those events, take some time to rededicate your life to Him. Remember that your eternal life isn't at stake, but your daily victory and the quality of your love relationship with God is.

2. *Close the door on sin.* Repentance means to turn away from sin and to hold onto God and His ways. Ask the Holy Spirit if there is any unconfessed sin in your life that you need to turn away from. (The Steps to Freedom in Christ available from our ministry will really help.)

3. *Destroy thoughts against God.* Sometimes we have expectations of God that are just not realistic. God is holy, righteous, and fair. There is no way we could ever word a prayer so that He would have to do our will. He is com-mitted to His own perfect character and He cannot sin. In addition, He is committed to always doing what is the very best for us. But when God doesn't do what we want, we sometimes harbor bitter thoughts against Him. Let the Lord reveal to your mind anything you might be holding against God. Let yourself get in touch with how you felt when things didn't go your way. Then destroy that thought against God.

4. *Remember that love is more than a feeling.* Love can be a great feeling, but that feeling can come and go. True love is *commitment.* You might be thinking, "But I don't *feel* like I love God." If you choose to love God and have turned from the sins that God has revealed to you, then you're in the right position to love God. The feeling of warmth and love will come in time. If you're not right with God, your love for Him will fade. But if you are radically right with God, regardless of how you feel, you're loving God.

5. *Keep God's commandments.* John 14:21 says, "Whoever has my commands and obeys them, he is the one who loves me. He who loves me will be loved by my Father, and I too will love him and show myself to him." Loving God means doing His will and following His Word. Loving means obeying.

More than a few years ago a young man by the name of Alexander the Great was running around the world conquering every country and kingdom he came across. He conquered almost all of the known world because he had the most committed army. His men were willing to go anywhere and do anything to win for their commander. The story goes that one day Alexander was out scouting around with only a small company of soldiers. He came upon on walled city that was well-defended. Alexander yelled up to the king and the men on the walls.

"Surrender to me at once!" commanded Alexander.

The king laughed. "Why should I surrender to you?" he called down. "We have you far outnumbered. You are no threat to us!"

Alexander was ready to answer the challenge. "Allow me to demonstrate why you should surrender," he replied. Alexander ordered his men to line up in single file and start marching. He marched them straight toward a sheer cliff that dropped hundreds of feet to rocks below.

The king and his soldiers watched in shock and disbelief as, one by one, Alexander's soldiers marched without hesitation right off the cliff to their deaths. After ten soldiers had died, Alexander ordered the rest of his men to return to his side.

The king and his soldiers surrendered on the spot to Alexander the Great.[1]

The king knew they wouldn't stand a chance against an army which was that committed to its leader.

Thankfully, Jesus doesn't ask us to jump off any cliffs, but He *does* ask us to obey Him. In fact, the roles are reversed: Our leader and commander Jesus is the One who died for *us*, so the least we can do is to obey His orders.

6. *Give God your worship, praise, and honor.* God is holy and awesome. He is worthy of all our praise and worship. The worship of God is so important that it actually goes on 24 hours a day in heaven. Listen to Revelation 4:8,9: "Each of the four living creatures had six wings and was covered with eyes all around, even under his wings. Day and night they never stop saying: 'Holy, holy, holy is the Lord God Almighty, who was, and is, and is to come.'... The living creatures give glory, honor and thanks to him who sits on the throne and who lives for ever and ever." Have you ever physically bowed down and told God how awesome He is?

LOVE LESSONS

Take some time right now and ask the Lord about your personal love relationship with him. How is your love for Him?

Use the six suggestions to restore the fullness of your first love for God. Start with number 1 and recall how you first felt after you accepted Christ.

In which one of those six areas did God seem to speak to you the most? Why do you think that area was brought to your attention?

THE LIE TO REJECT

I reject the lie that I am unable to love God or have a loving fellowship and personal relationship with Him.

THE TRUTH TO ACCEPT

I accept the truth that God loves me and that therefore I can love Him with all my heart, soul, mind, and strength.

PRAYER FOR TODAY

Dear heavenly Father, I want to keep my first love for You alive. I don't want to ever lose my first love for You. I choose to recall my first love for You and to close any doors I may have opened up to sin. Lord, I love You and want to obey You and worship You with a whole heart. Amen.

TODAY'S BIBLE READING

Proverbs 6:1-5
Theme: Don't be too sure

The Rewards of Love

We know that in all things God works for the good of those who love him, who have been called according to his purpose (Romans 8:28).

Love has its rewards. God actually promises that everything will work for the good for those who love Him. The problem is our understanding what is good for us. An old Chinese proverb tells of a young man who was raised in a peasant home. One day a stranger rode by his home leading several horses. He called out, "If there is a young man in the household, I would like to give him a horse!" Wow, the young man was given the most incredible gift someone in his poor background could possibly receive. What a great thing to have his own horse!

The next day as he was riding, he fell off the horse and broke his leg. Well, maybe owning a horse was not a good thing after all; maybe it was a bad thing. However, the following day some warlords came out of the hills and insisted the young man ride with them into war. But the boy could not go because he had a broken leg. Suddenly having a broken leg was a good thing!

The proverb continues on and on, alternating between what appeared to be a good thing one day, but turned out to be a bad thing the next day. The problem is that we really don't know what is good for us. God can work through anything. What is good is what God wills.

God does not promise to make a bad thing good, nor has He assured us that He will keep us from bad things. But He has promised us that in all things—even those that are terrible—good can come out of it for all those who *love Him*. In Romans 5:3-5 Paul states, "We also exult in our tribulations, knowing that tribulation brings about perseverance; and perseverance, proven character; and proven character, hope; and hope does not disappoint, because the love of God has been poured out within our hearts through the Holy Spirit who was given to us" (NASB).

In verse 3, "exult" means heightened joy; "tribulation" means to be under pressure; "perseverance" means to remain under pressure. As you first look at the verse, it may seem that God has it in for us! But that is a wrong view. God is simply trying to show us that in the midst of trials and tribulations He intends to produce the result of proven character, and that is where our hope lies.

Many young people today believe their life is worthless. Their solution? Check out! If their job is miserable, they change jobs. If their youth group has problems, they switch churches. They are running away from difficult situations, sometimes even literally running away and leaving town.

But trying to change other people or circumstances isn't where our hope lies. God's plan is that we hang in there and grow up. Our hope lies in our proven character, not in good times. Hope based on good times will always disappoint us, but hope based on the love of God and our proven character will never disappoint us.

Even so, we should be aware of false hopes. God never promised that everything would turn out exactly as we would like. Our hope is not in believing that life should be smooth sailing, and that if things are rough right now, they'll be better in the morning. Our hope lies in the fact that God will make us better people and conform us to His image *through* our difficult circumstances.

Suppose you came to us feeling like you were about to die because your boyfriend or girlfriend just broke up with you. You would be crying out for hope, and we would want to give you some. But if we said, "Oh, we'll get you two back together again," we would be giving you a false hope. We cannot promise that.

But we could say, "Listen, if you have not committed yourself in the past to be the best possible man or woman that God wants you to be, would you commit yourself to that right now?" Even if your relationship isn't restored, you could come through this tribulation with proven character. You can become a better person than you were before the crisis, and that's where your hope lies.

God knew us from the foundations of the world and picked us to be conformed to the likeness of His Son. In what way did He know us? Some Bible teachers strongly believe in divine election, which means God chose us to be His children from the beginning of time. They appeal to passages such as Ephesians 1:4,5: "He chose us in him before the creation of the world to be holy and blameless in his sight. In love he predestined us to be adopted as his sons through Jesus Christ, in accordance with his pleasure and will." Others believe salvation depends on a person's personal choice, citing verses such as Romans 10:13: "Everyone who calls on the name of the Lord will be saved."

Don't go to either extreme on this issue. One extreme sees divine election as if there is no involvement of the human will. The other extreme sees salvation solely as a matter of human choice. But God's control and human responsibility are *both* taught in the Word of God.

Someone has suggested that if we looked upon the gateway to eternal life from the outside we would see the sign "Whoever calls upon the name of the Lord shall be saved." But after we have called upon the name of the Lord and have walked through that gate, looking back we would see the inscription "You were known from the foundations of the world."

The important thing is to realize that we have been known and chosen from the foundation of the world. Even if this refers only to the fact that in eternity past God knew those who would by faith become His people we *were* nevertheless foreknown and chosen to be conformed to the image of God. That is what the "all things" of Romans 8:28 are working together to accomplish in our lives—that we take on the very character of Christ.

LOVE LESSONS

Why does God allow hard times to come into our lives? Why is it important to love God in the midst of them?

Why is it so important to recall that God loves us and handpicks us to be conformed to the image of Christ when trouble comes?

THE LIE TO REJECT

I renounce the lie that God has forsaken me during difficult times or that there is no hope.

The Truth to Accept

I accept the truth that God loves me and that He has a purpose in my life—to conform me to Christ's image.

Prayer for Today

Dear heavenly Father, I am in awe that You have known me from the beginning of time. I confess that I don't fully understand what that really means, for You alone are God. I accept Your purpose for my life to be conformed to Your image during times of trouble. Thank You for the hope this gives me and the assurance that in all things You work for good.

I renounce the lie of Satan that I must not be a Christian or not walking in the Spirit if bad things happen. I renounce the lie that You have forsaken me during difficult times or that there is no hope. I assume my responsibility to allow You to fulfill Your purpose in my life—to conform me to Your image. I ask for Your grace to enable me to be like Christ. I now profess that my hope lies in the knowledge that You are working through all the trials in my life to develop proven character. In Jesus' precious name I pray. Amen.

Today's Bible Reading

Proverbs 6:6-19
Theme: Don't get lazy

The Spirit of Love

The fruit of the Spirit is love, joy, peace, patience, kindness, goodness, faithfulness, gentleness and self-control. Against such things there is no law. Those who belong to Christ Jesus have crucified the sinful nature with its passions and desires (Galatians 5:22-24).

God is love, Jesus is love, the Holy Spirit is love. Why? Because they are all the same God in three Persons. The fruit of the Spirit is love. Have you ever asked yourself what a loving God looks like? Well, Galatians 5:22-24 gives us the answer. When we love God we will manifest a love that is visible to other people. Others will be able to see it and hear it. There will be joy, a smile, and a warm laugh. You can see joy. In fact it's hard to hide.

We all know the happiness that comes when things are going great. Let's say you just won a free trip to Walt Disney World—airfare, hotels, the works. I'm pretty sure you would express happiness and maybe even do a few cartwheels. But the fruit of the Spirit doesn't need some windfall to set it off. Christians who are being led by the Spirit have true joy regardless of how good or bad things are going. Do you manifest joy when you think about God? Do you have a sense of peace, that inner tranquility that lets you sleep soundly? Do you have patience and the strength to wait because you know God has the best in store for you?

God wants us to manifest these things because these are the qualities of God's character. When we are kind and good, we are showing people what God looks like. When we show faithfulness and gentleness, people around us will see Christ in us and ask us about the source of our peace. (If we lack self-control, people will think we are no different from other people who don't know Christ.) All of these qualities are signs of loving God and the fruit of the Spirit. We can't say we truly love God unless we see these fruits of the Spirit in our lives.

In his book *Mortal Lessons* (Touchstone Books, 1987) physician Richard Selzer describes a scene in a hospital room after he had performed surgery on a young women's face:

> I stand by the bed where the young woman lies.... her face, postoperative ... her mouth twisted in palsy ... clownish. A tiny twig of the facial nerve, one of the muscles of her mouth, has been severed. She will be that way from now on. I had followed with religious fervor the curve of her flesh, I promise you that. Nevertheless, to remove the tumor in her cheek, I had cut this little nerve. Her young husband is in the room. He stands on the opposite side of the bed, and together they seem to be in a world all their own in the evening lamplight ... isolated from me ... private.

> Who are they? I ask myself ... he and this wry mouth I have made, who gaze at and touch each other so generously. The young woman speaks. "Will my mouth always be like this?" she asks. "Yes," I say, "it will. It is because the nerve was cut." She nods and is silent. But the young man smiles. "I like it," he says. "It's kind of cute."

All at once I know who he is. I understand, and I lower my gaze. One is not bold in an encounter with the divine. Unmindful, he bends to kiss her crooked mouth, and I am so close I can see how he twists his own lips to accommodate to her . . . to show her that their kiss still works.[2]

God showed His great love for us by conforming Himself to the image of man and dying for our sin. We show our love for God by conforming to His commands. John 14:15 says, "If you love me, you will obey what I command." We love when we manifest the fruit of the Spirit. Saying we love God with our mouth is one thing, but letting other people see it through our genuine display of joy, peace, patience, and self control is another.

LOVE LESSONS

How have you displayed your love for God recently? Give an example.

Ask God to speak to you about the joy you have in your life. Is it joy from the world or inner joy from the Spirit? Ask Him about each of the qualities of the Holy Spirit.

Of all the qualities of the Spirit talked about in Galatians 5:22-24, which ones did God ask you to work on?

THE LIE TO REJECT

I renounce the lie that I am unable to display the fruit of the Spirit.

THE TRUTH TO ACCEPT

I accept the truth that God's Spirit lives in me and that I am able to experience God's love, joy, peace, patience, kindness, goodness, faithfulness, gentleness, and self-control.

PRAYER FOR TODAY

Dear heavenly Father, I want to display Your love, joy, peace, patience, kindness, goodness, faithfulness, gentleness, and self-control in my life. I know I can do this because Your Holy Spirit is so powerfully at work in my life. Thank You for indwelling me and filling me to the fullest measure with Your love. I want those around me to see Christ in me and ask why I'm so happy, why I have such peace. Help me point others to You. In Jesus' precious name I pray. Amen.

TODAY'S BIBLE READING

Proverbs 6:20-35
Theme: Avoid sexual sin

NOT A LOSER

*We are God's workmanship, created in Christ Jesus
to do good works, which God prepared in advance for
us to do* (Ephesians 2:10).

A young lady named Beth came to see me (Neil) who
was emaciated by anorexia, plagued by condemning
thoughts, and secretly cutting herself. Her parents were
climb-the-ladder professionals who would do anything for
their child—so long as it would produce the type of child
that would make them proud.

Beth had the best swimming and gymnastics coaches,
and her parents were pressuring her to attend a top-rated
secular school and join the best sorority (which, of course,
was the one her mother had belonged to). She wanted to
go to a Christian school, but even though her parents pro-
fessed to be Christians, they wouldn't allow it. They wanted
more for their child!

As I helped her through the Steps to Freedom, Beth
struggled to forgive her parents from her heart. "After all,
my folks are really good people, pillars of the community,"
she told me.

She hadn't cried in four years. Facing the need to forgive
her father, she said, "I think *I* need to ask *his* forgiveness."

"Maybe you do," I responded, "but we aren't dealing
with that right now. We are helping you find your freedom
in Christ by forgiving your father from your heart."

For several agonizing minutes she stared at the list of people she needed to forgive, then suddenly tears began to form in her eyes. "Lord, I forgive my father for never asking me what I would like to become and for disregarding my thoughts and feelings." The floodgate opened, and the freedom came.

The world puts a lot of pressure on us to conform to its image. Well-meaning parents often try to force their children to fit into their mold. Performance-based acceptance and cloning mentalities often produce what J. K. Summerhill calls a "loser's limp."

"Watch this," chuckled an athletic coach as we watched his track team compete in a high school athletic meet. "You see my boy there, coming in fourth? Limping! Chances are he just developed that limp to have an excuse for not doing better. I call it 'loser's limp.'" Some of the reasons why some men do not attain their goals—do not get one-tenth of the way to their goals—are no more convincing than the high school boy's suddenly developed limp. Worse yet, the loser's limp attitude may stop a man from even trying to lift his life above a subsistence level. When the gun goes off to start the race, he is licked before he starts.

He may put it to you earnestly: "You can see how badly I am handicapped by ..." and what follows is something defined as a handicap. Very rarely is it actually a handicap. Over and over, when some man tells me he is handicapped, I see a built-in loser's limp.

I am not talking about blind people, although one can still learn a wonderful lesson from Helen Keller. I am not talking about bedridden people, notwithstanding the fact that such men as James Royce, completely immobilized by polio, have built a thriving business from their beds. We should take off our hats to really handicapped people who still live constructive lives, but they are too exceptional for most of us to identify with.

I am talking, rather, about men who have the use of all their senses and all their limbs, surely the great majority of my readers. And perhaps I speak directly to you—if you have never taken charge of your life-dynamics; if you know that many and many another man, who has nothing you haven't got, is building a grand career and a glorious future while you get pushed into some low-level corner. If you've lost a few of life's races, see if you're not assuming you're a loser forever, if you're not acquiring a loser's limp before you start.

Check yourself for loser's limp right now![3]

Part of what Summerhill is talking about is not living up to our potential. The main reason we live at that level is that we get caught up in a false failure-success syndrome. The world's definition of success is to come in first, or to never fail. I saw a bumper sticker on a car that said, "If at first you don't succeed, then erase all possible evidence that you ever tried in the first place!" But to stumble and fall is not failure. To stumble and fall *again* is not failure. Failure is when you say, "I got pushed!"

The greatest failure in life is to never try. The only difference between a winner and a loser is that the winner gets up one more time than the loser. As Proverbs 24:16 says, "For though a righteous man falls seven times, he rises again, but the wicked are brought down by calamity." The loser may also be the timid soul who knows neither victory nor defeat because he never enters the race. Remember, a mistake is never a failure unless you fail to learn by it.

In the parable of the talents in Matthew 25:14-30, one of the slaves was given only one talent, which he took and buried. His idea of duty, progress, and stewardship was to slam on the brakes and throw the transmission into reverse! But God considered him a wicked slave. He should have taken the talent entrusted to him and invested it in the kingdom of God. The fearful person asks, "What do I stand to lose if I do?" A person of faith asks, "What do I stand to lose if I don't?"

Two types of people will never amount to anything: those who cannot do what they are told, and those who won't do anything *unless* they are told. In the parable, the slave with one talent had just as much responsibility as the one with five talents: Both were required to be submissive to the master. But one took the risk of doing while the other sought the security of hiding. I understand why people like to have the security of clinging to a tree trunk, but the fruit is always out on the end of the limb!

It's important to remember, however, that not everyone has the same level of giftedness. Maybe the young man in Summerhill's story had only the ability to come in fourth. Perhaps no matter what he did, or how hard he trained, the best he could ever do would be fourth place. What's wrong with that? In a four-man race, someone has to come in fourth!

We should seek to live up to our potential and not look for excuses, but not everybody's potential is the same. The Lord hasn't equally distributed gifts, talents or intelligence. But He has equally distributed Himself.

What makes up success, and whose expectations are we to live up to? God uses parents, pastors, and all the people we rub shoulders with to mold us into the person He wants us to be. But we are *God's* workmanship: not our parents', not our pastor's, not society's.

In Christ Jesus we can become the masterpiece He intended from the foundation of the world. That is the good work to which God has called us.

Love Lessons

What is loser's limp? Check yourself for loser's limp right now. Ask the Lord if you have any wrong beliefs about yourself.

Is everyone gifted with the same talents? Why is it important to recognize the world's false expectations and the Lord's real expectations?

Can everyone be successful? Explain.

The Lie to Reject

I renounce the lies of Satan that would compare me with others who are more gifted or less gifted than I am. I have everything I need to love God.

The Truth to Accept

I accept the truth that I have been given gifts, talents that God has entrusted to me. I choose to use them to show my love for God.

Prayer for Today

Dear heavenly Father, I praise You for knowing me and preparing me from the foundation of the world to have a love relationship with You. I don't fully understand that, but I do know I want to be Your divine masterpiece. I want to be all that You created me to be and to love You fully. I know that the good work You have called me to do can only come from who I am in Christ.

Forgive me for the times I have let others determine who I am and for the times I have tried to make others become what I wanted them to be. I refuse to believe the lie that says success is determined by the standards of this world. I renounce the lie that my success is found in my performance. I announce the truth that my success is found in being who You created me to be and doing what You called me to do.

Forgive me for not taking the risk of stepping out on faith according to what I know to be true. I commit myself to making full use of the gifts, talents, and other life endowments that You have entrusted to me. In Jesus' precious name I pray. Amen.

TODAY'S BIBLE READING

Proverbs 7:1-27
Theme: Avoid wild people

LOVING GOD, LOVING OTHERS

Dear friends, let us love one another, for love comes from God. Everyone who loves has been born of God and knows God. Whoever does not love does not know God, because God is love (1 John 4:7,8).

Loving God means loving others. I (Dave) travel a great deal and often find myself waiting at airports. Sometime it's frustrating when word comes over the intercom that the flight will be delayed because of weather or some kind of mechanical malfunction. Because I travel so much, I want to get home to my wife and kids as fast as possible.

On one occasion I found myself waiting for a delayed flight in Phoenix, Arizona. One hour passed by, and then two. I began to feel sorry for myself, thinking things like, "Lord, I've dedicated my life to You, so the least You could do is have a plane ready for me so I can go home!"

As the minutes passed, I got even more angry. Suddenly a man came through the door and went up to the airline desk. "One ticket please," he stammered as he pulled out a wad of wrinkled dollar bills. He didn't have a reservation. He looked terrible, like an escaped prisoner from Alcatraz. His hair was long and unwashed. He wasn't wearing a shirt—only a leather vest. His Levi pants were—well, let's say they were very broken in. Suddenly the airline stewardess said to him, "Sir, that flight is ready to board right now. You can board through Gate B. . . . Oh, by the way, Mr. Park, you may board as well." I know I shouldn't have thought this way, but this was the thought running through my head: "Lord, this guy is a pagan—he doesn't even know You—and the plane is ready for him. But Lord, I serve You, and You make me wait!" As we entered the plane I didn't feel like talking to anyone because I was still half angry. I just wanted to go home and be with my family.

The flight was a short 45-minute hop and we soon landed. As I made my way to my van I noticed that the biker dude was walking down the road with his suitcase in tow. I couldn't believe what I was about to do because I knew what this guy's real plan was. He would travel to some little town and get some idiot to pick him up, then whip out a chain saw from his suitcase and murder the guy.

I knew I was headed for a photo on the back of a milk carton, but I felt strongly that I should pick this guy up. His arms were huge and he was easily twice my weight. I stopped, rolled down the window, and asked him if he needed a ride. "Oh, yeah, man, thanks!" I stepped out of the van and picked up his suitcase and put it in the back. (It was heavy enough to be holding a chain saw.)

As I jumped back into the van I asked him where he was headed. He paused for a long time. "Well," he finally said, "I actually live about 15 miles out of town in the woods." There it was. He was going to take me out to the woods and I would be his next victim.

My martyrdom would have to wait, however, because as I turned the van around I noticed that he was weeping. He wasn't just weeping, but bawling. "Are you all right?"

I asked. "I'm sorry," he said, "but I just lost my job and there isn't a job to be found and my wife of 14 years just left me, and to top it all off I'm about to lose my home and land. The bank's about to foreclose on me."

I was stunned. This man looked so hard, so tough. I had no idea his heart was breaking. "Boy," I said softly, "it sounds to me like you need"—I paused, then I just said it—"*Jesus.*" "That's what I need," he shot back. "I need Jesus!" A few short moments earlier my life had been totally consumed with my own little world, but now I could see a divine appointment unfolding right beside me. Love—that's what this man needed.

As I shared Christ's love and His death on the cross, the big man asked the question every evangelist loves to hear: "What do I need to do to be saved?" As we reached his home and stepped outside the car, there in his front yard he gave his life to Christ.

A little love and compassion goes a long way. "Dear friends, let us love one another, for love comes from God. Everyone who loves has been born of God and knows God. Whoever does not love does not know God, because God is love" (1 John 4:7,8).

In addition to loving the lost, God wants us to love our brothers and sisters in Christ. John 13:35 reminds us, "By this all men will know that you are my disciples, if you love one another." Loving isn't always easy because it means putting someone else's needs before yours. I wanted to go home right away, but because I took a little time and showed a little love, that man's eternal destiny was forever changed. When we love, especially each other, the whole world takes note and recognizes us as followers of Jesus.

Love Lessons

Why is loving each other so important? What happens if we don't?

Take some time to recall a situation when you were able to demonstrate love for someone else. How did it make the person feel?

How did you feel when someone demonstrated love for you? How did you feel about him or her?

The Lie to Reject

I renounce the lie of Satan that I am unable to love others.

The Truth to Accept

I accept the truth that God has created a new heart of love in me and that I am able to love like Jesus loved because His Spirit is alive in me.

Prayer for Today

Dear heavenly Father, I praise You for loving me. I know that the world will see Christ in me and will know that I am one of Your followers when I choose to love with Christlike love. I choose to love the lost and not become unapproachable. I also choose to love my fellow brothers and sisters in Christ. I choose to think of them and their needs and put them before my own personal needs. In Jesus' name I pray. Amen.

Today's Bible Reading

Proverbs 8:1-21
Theme: What is wisdom?

PART FOUR

Love and Friendships

A True Friend

A righteous man is cautious in friendship, but the way of the wicked leads them astray (Proverbs 12:26).

We all need to be affirmed, loved, and accepted. Family and friends are important, and we need their guidance in our lives. But these hold second place to Someone! Nothing can compare or replace what Christ alone provides in terms of acceptance, security, and significance.

When we get our main affirmation from a source other than Christ we become a wide-open target. It won't be long until the damaging arrows of peer pressure hit the bull's-eye and we compromise our purity.

If you understand who you are in Christ and know that your identity is found *in Him,* it's far easier to stand against the pressures you face. If, however, your identity is coming from a source other than Christ, it's just a matter of time before the world, the flesh or the devil pressure you into compromising what you know is right.

When it comes to purity, our foundation must be a rock-solid understanding of who we are in Christ. Then we must build upon that foundation by establishing godly friendships. Our friendships are one of the strongest guiding forces in our lives, either a force for good or a force for evil.

What is a true friend? A true friend provides loyalty, devotion, and support. He or she takes you into his confidence. It's a two-sided relationship where both of you share and give of yourselves. For a true friendship to take place you must see yourself as a child of God and see other believers as "in Christ" as well. Otherwise you just become acquaintances and never companions.

At our conferences we often ask the question, "In the short time we are together, if we really got to know you, would we like you?" Then we always respond, "I'm sure we would." Without exception, this is true of the people we have come to know intimately, even if they have trouble relating socially or are afraid of getting close to others. After hearing the difficulties from their pasts, we find that as a result of knowing them we come to enjoy them and love them.

But developing friendships is risky. You have to open yourself up to others and be real! It's true that no one person apart from Christ can meet all our emotional needs. But without taking the risk of opening up to a trusted friend, you never develop the intimacy you so desperately want and need.

Freedom and responsibility walk hand in hand. One of the most important responsibilities we have as believers is the proper selection of our friends. There is no better way to enhance our walk of freedom than to select sound friendships. If we select poor friends, however, bondage is usually not far away. Proverbs 12:26 says, "A righteous man is cautious in friendship, but the way of the wicked leads them astray."

God wants us to focus on developing our own character while seeking to meet the needs of those around us. "Do nothing out of selfish ambition or vain conceit, but in humility consider others better than yourselves. Each of you should look not only to your own interests, but also to the interests of others. Your attitude should be the same as

that of Christ Jesus" (Philippians 2:3-5). That's the way to
have a godly friendship.

Love Lessons

Take some time to let the Lord reveal the truth about your
current friendships. Are they helping or hurting your relationship with God? Also let Him reveal to you the kind of
friend He wants *you* to be.

Do your friends build you up or tear you down spiritually?

Is it more important to you that your friends like you or is
it more important that you please God? Why?

Are you looking to your friends alone to meet your need
for acceptance, security, and significance?

The Lie to Reject

*I renounce the lie that I can find perfect acceptance, secu-
rity and significance in my human friendships apart from
Christ.*

The Truth to Accept

*I accept the truth that God has accepted me because He
loves me, and that I am accepted, secure and significant
because I belong to Him.*

PRAYER FOR TODAY

Dear heavenly Father, I want You to be in control of my relationships. Help me to select good friends that will build me up in my faith. I choose to look to You alone for my acceptance, security, and significance. I know that I belong to You. Help me to spot any friendships that the enemy might use to hurt me. I want to close any door of opportunity the enemy may have to get to me. Help me to select my friends prayerfully and carefully. In Jesus' name I pray. Amen.

TODAY'S BIBLE READING

Proverbs 8:22-31
Theme: Where does wisdom come from?

Being a Real Friend

A friend loves at all times . . . (Proverbs 17:17).

There are ten important qualities in real friendship. We'll cover five of them today and the other five tomorrow. The first one of these is *communication.*

1. A real friend will communicate. Communication can be tricky. As the old saying goes, *"I know you believe you understand what I think I said, but I'm not sure you realize that what you heard is not what I meant."* Communication is the key link in the chain of friendship. A friendship will never grow and develop if the communication is bad.

Many friendships are just at the casual stage: You talk but you really don't say much. You haven't built up any trust yet, so you're careful about what you share. It involves shallow conversation like "How are you?" or "Did you hear the new Steven Curtis Chapman CD?"

Stage 2 is cliché communication. You talk about others, what they did or said, but not much about yourself. The conversation about yourself usually relates only to what you did or said. There is personal conversation but you're not about to tell this person your deepest fears or secret struggles.

Stage 3 is close communication, which involves revealing to others how you really feel about something. You reveal your true opinions, hopes, fears, needs and secrets. Many friendship never reach Stage 3.

Communication Stages

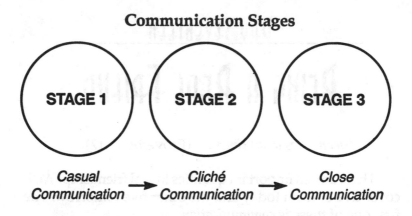

Casual Communication → Cliché Communication → Close Communication

2. A real friend is compatible. You can't be a real friend to someone you're not compatible with. Friendships are usually formed with someone you get along with well and have something in common with. You like to do the same things and have similar goals and desires.

The first place to look is for your compatibility with others is in the area of *beliefs.* Compatibility in beliefs doesn't just mean that you're both Christians but also that you have the same convictions. Your best friends ought to be believers. If they aren't believers, their capacity to be a friend to you is greatly hindered. Remember, only a believer has the loving presence of the Holy Spirit to guide and direct him in life.

Do nonbelievers have different goals and desires than most Christians? Sadly yes, because they lack the guidelines of God's Word and a personal relationship with God. Your friends will influence your belief system either for good or for bad. The question you need to ask yourself is, Do I want to become what that person is like? Proverbs 17:4

gives us the straight truth: "A wicked man listens to evil lips; a liar pays attention to a malicious tongue."

3. *A real friend develops others.* As a true friend, you must focus on loving and developing others. As you do, you'll find that you're also helping to develop yourself. As a Christian friend you are called to help others grow in their love and walk with Jesus. That makes you a developer.

In photography a developer uses chemicals to make a picture on unexposed film become visible. Your job as a Christian developer isn't much different: You're called to help others see themselves as "in Christ" and to grow in their walk of freedom with Him. Like the unexposed film that has the picture already on it, it's just waiting to be developed. So, too, you and your Christian friends are just waiting to be developed.

In your friendships, however, do you have your own interests at heart or the other person's? Many guys become friends with a girl only to attempt a sexual conquest. What's your motivation? Is it sexual or is it to develop godly character? We must be the kind of friends who will stand by others in their lowest moments, and, if God gives us the opportunity, sacrifice ourselves to help meet their needs.

For someone to qualify as your friend, does he or she have to be popular or good-looking or come from the right family and be wealthy? If that's required of your friends, Jesus would never have qualified as your friend! Proverbs 17:17 reminds us, "A friend loves at all times."

4. *A real friend accepts others.* As a believer you must see yourself as a child of God (John 1:12). If you don't accept a Christian friend for who he is in Christ, even with all of his or her strengths and weaknesses, you will always be trying to change him. But changing someone is the Holy Spirit's job. We are to accept others just as they are. Romans 15:7

says, "Accept one another, then, just as Christ accepted you, in order to bring praise to God."

Look to Christ to meet your needs in the way He chooses. "My God will meet all your needs according to his glorious riches in Christ Jesus" (Philippians 4:19). A friendship can't withstand the pressures of unacceptance. Without true acceptance it's just a matter of time before the relationship will crumble.

Of course, accepting others doesn't mean you go along with your friends if they are sinning. You are never called to compromise your character. Jesus loved and accepted sinners, but He Himself never sinned. He never changed what He believed or how He behaved.

5. *A real friend is trustworthy.* A true friendship is characterized by trust and loyalty. If someone opens up to you and tells you a deeply personal feeling or event, do you laugh at him, or worse yet, blab it to others? Trustworthiness means keeping a confidence. One of the key ingredients to a sound friendship is trust. Others need to know that your lips are sealed, that their feelings and thoughts won't be broadcast all over town. "A perverse man stirs up dissension, and a gossip separates close friends" (Proverbs 16:28).

In our youth leadership conferences we often ask people to write down their deepest, darkest secret. Most wouldn't write anything. Then we ask them if they would be willing to share what they wrote. Most say, "No way!" We really didn't want them to write anything on the paper. Then we ask them to write down the qualities of the person they would be willing to tell their secrets to. Then we ask them, Are you like that person? What they write on their paper usually describes God. On almost everyone's list is the word "trustworthy."

Love Lessons

I am influenced by my friends to do things I know are wrong.

Circle one:

Almost always   Sometimes   Seldom   Never

Do you ever hang around with certain people so others will think you're popular even though you know they are not really your friends?

List the names of the friends that you can really trust and that are truly loyal to you.

Have you ever closed the door to a true friendship because you thought it would make you unpopular with others? Has anyone ever closed the door on you? Explain?

The Lie to Reject

I renounce the lie that I have to compromise who I am in Christ to have good friends.

The Truth to Accept

I accept the truth that will lead me to the right kind of friendships and help me spot the false friendships that the enemy may try to set me up with.

Prayer for Today

Dear heavenly Father, I look to You to conform me to the image of Your Son, Jesus. I want to be a true friend to others by communicating well with them. I choose to let people in, to let them see the real me. As they see me, Lord, I hope they see that You are at work in my Life. Help me, Lord, to develop others and accept them as they are without compromising my walk with You. I want to be a friend to others the way Jesus is a friend to me. In Jesus' name I pray. Amen.

Today's Bible Reading

Proverbs 8:32-36
Theme: Those who are wise

Day Eighteen

More on Being a Real Friend

As iron sharpens iron, so one man sharpens another
(Proverbs 27:17).

Let's pick up where we left off yesterday. We've already covered communication, compatibility, developing others, acceptance, and trustworthiness. Today we'll cover five more qualities of true friendship. Remember, these qualities all work together. You don't want just one or two of them in your friendships—you want all of them.

6. A real friend is an encouragement. As a true friend you will lead and counsel others in the ways of the Lord. Proverbs 27:9, says "Oil and perfume make the heart glad; so a man's counsel is sweet to his friend" (NASB). Ask God for the wisdom to know how to listen and empathize with others. A godly friend is one who has learned the art of seeing things from God's point of view and not losing biblical truth in the midst of bad circumstances.

Be a friend who will lift and encourage others—one who laughs with them instead of at them and who cries with them instead of hurting them. Be a friend who knows when to offer helpful words of advice and when to be present but silent.

7. A real friend sacrifices himself for others. Jesus said, "For even the Son of Man did not come to be served, but to serve, and to give his life as a ransom for many" (Mark 10:45). Satan doesn't really believe that we are capable of living the self-sacrificing life. He believes that we are all basically selfish and interested only in what pleases us. Our new life in Christ, however, has made it possible for us to fulfill the servant-oriented life that Christ was able to live out before us.

Jesus calls us to follow His example, but too often we only want what we can get out of a friendship. A true friend may be called upon to sacrifice money and something even more valuable: time. Often the value of something is determined by what it costs you. God invested everything to have a friendship with you. It cost Him His Son! "My command is this: Love each other as I have loved you. Greater love has no one than this, that he lay down his life for his friends" (John 15:12,13).

8. A real friend strengthens others. As a true friend you will help others live out a positive Christian witness and testimony. Proverbs 27:17 says, "As iron sharpens iron, so one man sharpens another." Jesus sent out His disciples two by two for just this reason. Your closest friends should be believers.

It's not that we should become Christian snobs; we are to always reach out to the lost (Acts 1:8). But those who haven't accepted Christ as their Savior don't possess the Holy Spirit and can only imitate true love. True love can only come from God and can only be displayed in fullness by a person who is indwelt by the Spirit of God.

So don't look to non-Christians for strength, since they don't have anything to draw from. James 4:4 reminds us, "Don't you know that friendship with the world is hatred toward God? Anyone who chooses to be a friend of the world becomes an enemy of God." We are to be a source of strength to others through prayer and loving support. We are not, however, called to compromise our beliefs or behavior to satisfy our friends. Rather, we are actually called to avoid bad company (Proverbs 1:8-19).

9. *A real friend is honest with others.* Satan is by his very nature a liar. He would love nothing more than for your relationships with your friends to be riddled with deceptions and lies. Ephesians 4:15 says, "Instead, speaking the truth in love, we will in all things grow up into him who is the Head, that is, Christ." Learn how to share how you really feel and what you really think.

Too often we're afraid to tell others what we really believe because we think others will ridicule us. But if they can't accept us and our beliefs, then they really aren't our friends. True friendship and understanding come on the coattails of honesty. Can you share who you are in Christ with your current friends? Or is your Christianity a secret thing? They need what you have, so don't be tricked by the enemy into not sharing it!

10. *A real friend forgives others.* Being a real friend means forgiving others. You won't travel too far down the road of friendship before you get hurt and hurt others.

We are to forgive as Christ has forgiven us (Ephesians 4:32). When Jesus forgave us, He agreed to take upon Himself the consequences of our sin. He will not use our past offenses against us. And that's what Jesus is asking us to do too. "He who covers an offense promotes love, but whoever repeats the matter separates close friends" (Proverbs 17:9).

In helping teens find their freedom in Christ, we've come to see that unforgiveness is the number one problem among youth. Satan loves it when Christians fight or harbor grudges and separate one another. Make the choice to forgive.

Love Lessons

How do you encourage your Christian friends who know Christ in their walk with Jesus? How do you encourage those who don't know Christ?

Have you ever lied to your friends because you think that's what they wanted to hear? Have you ever been lied to? If that happened, how did it make you feel?

Have you ever refused to forgive a friend who has hurt you, even though you know God wants you to? Is there anyone the Lord wants you to forgive right now?

The Lie to Reject

I renounce the lie of Satan that I can't be a real friend and encouragement to others.

The Truth to Accept

I accept the truth that God has given me the ability through the Holy Spirit to be a real friend and an encouragement to all those that God brings into my life.

Prayer for Today

Lord, what an encouragement You are to me! I want to build others up, so I'm willing to sacrifice my desires to help others see You. I choose to be honest. I choose to speak the truth in love. Lord, I don't want to ignore Your voice when I sense You are telling me to share with others. I also choose to forgive those who hurt me and not to let any bitterness or unforgiveness come between me and the friends you have given me. In Jesus' name I pray. Amen.

Today's Bible Reading

Proverbs 9:1-18
Theme: The fool

DAY NINETEEN

YOUR BEST FRIEND

He who loves a pure heart and whose speech is gracious will have the king for his friend (Proverbs 22:11).

In addition to being a good friend you also need good friends. You will naturally want friends who display the qualities we talked about the last two days. These were the very qualities that attracted me (Dave) to my wife, Grace. (Not to mention her great humor, looks, and intelligence!) You will find that as you develop these qualities, people will be attracted to you and want to be your friend.

You also need a true friend who might become a lifelong friend and lover, an intimate companion and mate. You need true friends in order to look for a mate. "Then the Lord God said, 'It is not good for the man to be alone. I will make him a helper suitable for him' " (Genesis 2:18). "For this cause a man shall leave his father and his mother and shall cleave to his wife; and they shall become one flesh" (Genesis 2:24 NASB). Remember you may end up marrying someone who is a friend first, so select your friends carefully.

In Christ you have the best friend you could ever have. Many others may desert you during times of trouble, but Jesus invites you to draw near to Him. In John 15:12-17 He says that you are no longer a servant, doing only what is commanded without understanding the purpose. Jesus takes His friends into His confidence.

In John 15:15 He says, "Everything that I learned from my Father I have made known to you." He also said, "But when he, the Spirit of truth, comes, he will guide you into all truth.... All that belongs to the Father is mine. That is why I said the Spirit will take from what is mine and make it known to you" (John 16:13,15). Jesus discloses Himself to us ... we know Him ... He invites us to draw near ... He is the friend who sticks closer than a brother, the One who stays with us through all adversity.

Another proof that Jesus is your best friend is that He purposely gave Himself for you. He sacrificed Himself to meet your greatest need. "This is how we know what love is: Jesus Christ laid down his life for us" (1 John 3:16). Many people express the sentiment, "Oh, I wish Jesus was my friend." That wish has already been granted. He is your friend because He chose to be your friend; He chose you.

Have you ever wished that a certain person in your life would be your friend? Perhaps you thought, "I'm going to do whatever I can to make him my friend," only to be disappointed because he had his own agenda and didn't share your desire for friendship. But consider what you already have. We are talking about the God of the universe—the most "significant other" that you could possibly have in your life. And He chose you!

You may say, "I know Jesus is my friend, but how can I be a friend to Jesus?" First of all, let's go back to what makes a friend. The most important thing you can do is be real with God. Open yourself up to Him, be totally honest, walk in the light, and unburden yourself before Him, knowing that He loves you and has your best interests at heart.

The book of Matthew also reminds us that when we love others we are also showing love toward God. "The King will reply, 'I tell you the truth, whatever you did for one of the least of these brothers of mine, you did for me'" (Matthew 25:40).

The story is told of one man's life who just watched others love but never let people get close enough to experience love himself.

> He saw people love each other, and he saw that love makes strenuous demands on the lovers. He saw that love required sacrifice and self-denial. He saw that love produced arguments, jealousy, and sorrow. He decided that love cost too much. He decided not to diminish his life with love.
>
> He saw people strive for distant and hazy goals. He saw men strive for success and women strive for high ideals. He saw that the striving was often mixed with disappointment. He saw strong and committed men fail, and he saw weak, undeserving men succeed. He saw that striving sometimes forced people into pettiness and greed. He decided that it cost too much. He decided not to soil his life with striving.
>
> He saw people serving others. He saw men give money to the poor and helpless. He saw that the more they served, the faster the need grew. He saw ungrateful receivers turn on their serving friends. He decided not to soil his life with serving.
>
> When he died, he walked up to God and presented his life to Him—undiminished, unmarred, unsoiled. The man was clean and untouched by the filth of the world, and he presented himself to God proudly saying, "Here is my life!"
>
> And God said, "Life? *What life?*"[1]

We love God best by loving others. Loving others can hurt, though, since people don't always love you back. They didn't return Jesus' love either. In fact, they were so jealous of Him that they crucified Him. His only crime was that He dared to love the unlovely.

LOVE LESSONS

What are some of the proofs that Jesus is your best friend?

When you stand before Jesus, what do you think He will say about your life, your friendships, and the way you loved?

In what way have you shown your love for Jesus by loving others? Give some examples.

How does knowing that Jesus is your best friend help you love others?

THE LIE TO REJECT

I renounce the lie that I can love God but not love others.

THE TRUTH TO ACCEPT

I accept the truth that God wants me to demonstrate my great love for Him by reaching out and loving others regardless of how they treat me.

PRAYER FOR TODAY

Dear Jesus, I know that when You walked on this earth and demonstrated Your great love for mankind You were rejected, mistreated, and killed. Yet You never stopped loving even those who were unlovely and evil. I want to be like You and show You how much I love You by reaching out and loving the unlovely. Thank You for Your friendship. It helps me to know that You are always there for me even when I am rejected by others. I know that I will never be rejected by You. In Your name I pray. Amen.

TODAY'S BIBLE READING

Proverbs 10:1-32
Theme: Good versus evil: round one

Forgiving Yourself

Therefore, there is now no condemnation for those who are in Christ Jesus (Romans 8:1).

God has forgiven everyone who has trusted Christ: "Therefore, there is now no condemnation for those who are in Christ Jesus" (Romans 8:1). Many Christians do not realize that they must also forgive themselves. Only God can forgive us for our sins, and we need to accept that forgiveness. Without that, it is very difficult to forgive and love others. When you forgive yourself, you are simply agreeing with God and receiving His forgiveness.

When one counselor suggested to a woman that she forgive herself for having an abortion, she suddenly came under great spiritual attack. She had already asked God's forgiveness, but forgiving herself was obviously where Satan wanted to keep her in bondage. After she forgave herself, the harassment she had lived with for so long stopped. The day after her appointment she approached the counselor again and said, "My mind has never been so quiet and peaceful."

Another young lady wrote:

Dear Dave and Neil,

For five agonizing years I was overcome with feelings of self-hatred, falling into anorexia, which eventually lead to bulimia and laxative abuse. I never thought I would conquer these obstacles. I began to refuse all thoughts of help and was conformed to my way of life.

Then my youth pastor gave me a copy of *The Bondage Breaker*, Youth Edition. I must admit, I read the first six chapters without much conviction. Finally one night something in my head snapped. I recognized in my mind after so many years, that I really did want to get well. I completed the book and dedicated my life to Christ.

Now I have found a fulfillment and a contented heart through the love of Christ. Learning that my life should be lived for the Lord, and not the world, has provided me with unimaginable joyfulness. Everything I do is now done with willingness and a joyful heart. I no longer seek the approval of others. Happiness and love for the Lord have consumed my heart. After suffering for so many years, I managed to break the bondage. Thank you for this inspirational book. It led me to the most important aspect of my life.

Very sincerely,

Jackie

As Jackie confessed and renounced the areas of her life that she had opened herself up to—the influence of world, the flesh, and the devil—she found freedom. Just as Christ forgave her, she was able to forgive herself and experience the joy and happiness that is every Christian's birthright.

Because you're Christ's friend, choose to love Him back by obeying Him. And by His grace, God will enable you to bear fruit and to love others.

LOVE LESSONS

Do you ever feel like the enemy has targeted your friendships?

Why is forgiving yourself so important? How does forgiving yourself relate to loving others?

What would happen if you didn't forgive yourself?

How did you feel when you read the two testimonies of the ladies that learned to forgive themselves? How could you relate to them?

THE LIE TO REJECT

I renounce the lie of Satan that I am unable to forgive myself.

THE TRUTH TO ACCEPT

I accept the truth that because God has forgiven me I can forgive myself.

PRAYER FOR TODAY

Dear heavenly Father, You have said in Your Word, "There is now no condemnation for those who are in Christ." I believe what Your Word says. I know that You will never punish me for my sin because Jesus bore the punishment for me. I choose to accept Your forgiveness and forgive myself so that I might not have anything hindering me from loving others. In Jesus' name I pray. Amen.

TODAY'S BIBLE READING

Proverbs 11:10-31
Theme: Good versus evil: round two

Part Five

Love and Dating

Part Five

Love and Dating

THE DATING TRAP

Seek first his kingdom and his righteousness, and all these things will be given to you as well (Matthew 6:33).

We all have the fear that we'll never be loved. So our hearts often become over anxious and we say yes before asking the right questions or before finding out a person's true motives or letting him or her become a friend first. Most people get in trouble in the area of sexuality because they don't have a planned date and they don't select their friends and dates prayerfully. Some will even go on blind dates. One classic blind date story goes like this.

> Since I was a little shy when I was in high school, I didn't ask many girls out on dates. So my friend came up to me one day and said, "Hey, I've lined you up with a great date for Saturday night. It's all set."
>
> "Who is it?" I asked. It turned out to be his cousin Doris. I had never met her. In fact, I had never met any girl named Doris. "Oh no," I said, "I'm not going on a blind date."
>
> "Hey, don't worry about this one," my friend said. "Doris is a terrific girl. And trust me—she's a real looker. But if you don't believe me, I'll tell you how to get out of the date if you don't like the way she looks. This is what I do: I go to a girl's front door to pick her up, and when she opens the door, I check her out. If I like what

I see, then great, we're all set. But if she's ugly, I fake an asthma attack. I go 'Aaahhhhgggggg!' (Hold your throat like you're having trouble breathing.) The girl asks, 'What's wrong?' And I say, 'It's my asthma.' And so we have to call off the date. Just like that. No problem."

"Well, I don't know ... but okay, it sounds easy enough. I'll do it," I said.

So I went to pick up Doris. I knocked on the door, and she came to the front door. I took a look at her, and to my surprise, my friend was right. She was beautiful! I stood there not knowing exactly what to say.

She took one look at me and went, "Aaahhhhggggg!"[1]

Some people get caught in the "I just have to be dating" trap. When I (Dave) was in high school and even in college most of my friends thought they had to be dating. If you weren't dating, people treated you like you had some kind of disease. But the Lord doesn't want us to seek dating, He wants us to seek Him. He doesn't want us to be obsessed about any relationship except the relationship we have with Him.

Jesus said, "Do not worry, saying,'What shall we eat?' or 'What shall we drink?' or 'What shall we wear?' For the pagans run after all these things, and your heavenly Father knows that you need them. But seek first his kingdom and his righteousness, and all these things will be given to you as well. Therefore do not worry about tomorrow, for tomorrow will worry about itself. Each day has enough trouble of its own" (Matthew 6:31-34).

I believe Jesus would say today, "Don't spend your time seeking a date and worrying about if you'll get to date. The unbelievers run after those things. Besides, your heavenly Father knows you need friendships and desire a mate.

But seek **first** your Father's plans for you and His kingdom and all these things will be given to you when you're ready for them and need them. So don't spend time worrying about who you're going to date tomorrow. Tomorrow will be filled with enough trouble. Why add to it?"

Matthew reminds us that we are to seek God's kingdom first. What does it mean to seek God's kingdom? It means to put the Lord's plans ahead of your own plans, to let Him call the shots and determine what goes on in your life— even who you date.

In the ancient Hebrew culture people didn't date! In fact the man and woman didn't even get to pick who they would marry; the man's father selected the bride. I don't think any of us want to go back to those days, but let's not miss the point: God, our heavenly Father, wants to pick who we date and who we marry. We're seeking God's kingdom when we let Him choose who we date. If you think about it, it's not that risky because God knows our needs and desires and wants to give us what is really best for us.

Love Lessons

Why do you think some people feel like they just have to be dating someone?

Why do you think people treat others who aren't dating like something is wrong with them?

Are you content or happy even if you're not dating someone? Explain.

What does it mean to seek God's kingdom first?

THE LIE TO REJECT

I renounce the lie that I can't trust God with my dating life.

THE TRUTH TO ACCEPT

I accept the truth that God knows what is best for me. So I choose to seek first God's kingdom and trust Him to meet my needs by bringing the right relationships into my life.

PRAYER FOR TODAY

Dear heavenly Father, I don't want to spend my time seeking a date and worrying about if I'll get to date. I know that unbelievers run after those things. Lord, I know that You understand my need for friendships and my desire for a mate. But I choose to seek first Your plans and Your kingdom. Help me, Lord, to be content with whatever circumstances I have in my life. I choose to live for You and trust in You. In Jesus' name I pray. Amen.

TODAY'S BIBLE READING

Proverbs 12:1-28
Theme: Good versus evil: round three

The Desires of Your Heart

Delight yourself in the LORD and he will give you the desires of your heart (Psalm 37:4).

To be delighted in the Lord means that you look to God alone to get your sense of security and belonging. It means that you look to Jesus to fulfill your need for love and acceptance. The real question isn't who are you going to date but who are you? Not what's your dating relationship like but what's your relationship with Jesus like?

Let's look a little closer at Psalm 37 and some of the verses that follow verse 4. Psalm 37:4-7 says:

> Delight yourself in the LORD and he will give you the desires of your heart. Commit your way to the LORD; trust in him and he will do this: He will make your righteousness shine like the dawn, the justice of your cause like the noonday sun. Be still before the LORD and wait patiently for him; do not fret when men succeed in their ways, when they carry out their wicked schemes.

God wants us to seek His righteousness. That means God wants us to live out our lives the same way Jesus lived out His. Jesus depended totally on his Father ("Father... not my will but yours be done"—Luke 22:42). Right now you might be thinking "Yeah, God probably won't let me date until I'm thirty!" If that's really a concern, then ask for God's help. Philippians says, "Do not be anxious about anything, but in everything, by prayer and petition, with thanksgiving, present your requests to God. And the peace of God, which transcends all understanding, will guard your hearts and your minds in Christ Jesus (Philippians 4:6,7).

But also be patient. A little later in the same portion of Scripture Paul says, "I have learned to be content whatever the circumstances" (Philippians 4:11). Let your heart be satisfied with the knowledge that God has things under control. He hasn't forgotten you and He knows just what you want and need.

Be patient—don't get in a rush. Take time to get to know a person before you even consider dating him or her. Ask the right questions. Has he trusted in Christ? Is he right with God and currently walking in fellowship with Him? What's his motive? Why does he want to date? If you get the wrong answers say, "I'm sorry, I know things wouldn't work out." Don't be rude, but speak the truth in love. If he asks you why you won't date him, tell him. Shoot straight. It may lead him to Christ or back to Christ.

Don't compromise; accept nothing less than God's best. First Corinthians 13:4-7 reminds us: "Love is patient, love is kind. It does not envy, it does not boast, it is not proud. It is not rude, it is not self-seeking, it is not easily angered, it keeps no record of wrongs. Love does not delight in evil but rejoices with the truth. It always protects, always trusts, always hopes, always perseveres." Don't let the enemy steal your hope. Trust God to provide the companionship and friendship you need, and then take initiative to love one another as He has loved you.

LOVE LESSONS

When you read Psalm 37:4, how does it make you feel?

Why do you think God's Word reminds us to be patient? How does that apply specifically to your dating life right now?

Have you ever felt like it was more important to you that you date than it was to please God? Why or why not?

Are you looking to your dating to meet your need for acceptance, security, significance, and a sense of belonging? Take some time and ask the Lord if you are.

THE LIE TO REJECT

I renounce the lie of Satan that the only way to find true acceptance, significance, security, and a sense of belonging is by dating.

THE TRUTH TO ACCEPT

I accept the truth that in Christ I am accepted, significant, and secure, and I belong to Him. Therefore I choose to give the Lord total control of my dating life.

PRAYER FOR TODAY

Dear heavenly Father, I want You to be in control of my dating life. Help me to patiently select or accept good dates that will build me up in my faith. I choose to look to You alone for my acceptance, security, and significance. I know I belong to You. Help me to spot any bad dates that the enemy might use to hurt me. I want to close any door of opportunity the enemy may have to get to me through my dating. Help me select my dates prayerfully and carefully. In Jesus' name I pray. Amen.

Today's Bible Reading

Proverbs 13:1-25
Theme: Good versus evil: round four

DANGEROUS AND DEADLY DATING

*I have hidden your word in my heart that I might not
sin against you* (Psalm 119:11).

One of the questions we get asked all the time is "Can
I date a non-Christian?" Well, nowhere in the Bible is there
a verse that says, "Thou shalt not date an unsaved person
or your brain will melt." However, God's Word does say:

> Do not be yoked together with unbelievers. For
> what do righteousness and wickedness have in
> common? Or what fellowship can light have with
> darkness? What harmony is there between Christ
> and Belial? What does a believer have in common
> with an unbeliever? What agreement is there
> between the temple of God and idols? For we are
> the temple of the living God. As God has said: "I
> will live with them and walk among them, and
> I will be their God, and they will be my people.
> Therefore come out from them and be separate,
> says the Lord. Touch no unclean thing, and I will
> receive you. I will be a Father to you, and you
> will be my sons and daughters, says the Lord
> Almighty" (2 Corinthians 6:14-18).

God doesn't leave us in the dark when it comes to marriage. He makes it very clear that we are not to marry an
unbeliever, because we don't have anything in common
with them spiritually. If we are not to marry an unbeliever,

why would you want to date one? Why risk falling in love with him or her?

Sadly, we have run into many people, usually women, who fell in love with an unsaved person. Almost all of them said they thought they could change him or lead him to Christ. You need to understand that your future husband or wife is going to come from who you date. You're probably saying, "Wow, that's real profound." But if you think about it, it's a strong motivation not to date unbelievers.

When God asks us to "come out from them," that doesn't mean we never talk to unsaved people. We are called to witness to them (Acts 1:8), but we need to be careful not to be negatively influenced by them.

You need to wait until you are mature enough to handle dating. Maturity is not just a physical age issue; it also has to do with how well you follow Christ. How well do people see Christ in you? Some people are in their thirties and still not ready to date.

Dangerous dating is when you run one of the red lights by dating too early, dating a non-Christian, or going on an unplanned date. If you run all three of these red lights you've moved into deadly dating. Though the Bible doesn't say specifically, "Don't date a non-Christian," it does give us examples of people who thought they could run the romantic red light and not get hurt. But they were tragically wrong.

Samson was a man in the Bible who really struggled with sexual sin, and it literally cost him his life. It isn't too hard for us to relate to his circumstances now that we live in the age of AIDS.

Samson was the strongest man in the Old Testament. You may recall some of the stories about him, but do you remember what his first biblically quoted words are? In brief, those words are, "I saw a woman" (Judges 14:2). We don't have to spend too much time wondering what was on his mind!

Apparently Samson didn't know much about starting a friendship because as soon as he returned to his parents from an out-of-town trip he said, "I have seen a Philistine woman in Timnah; now get her for me as my wife" (Judges 14:2). How romantic! "His father and mother replied, 'Isn't there an acceptable woman among your relatives or among all our people? Must you go to the uncircumcised Philistines to get a wife?' But Samson said to his father, 'Get her for me. She's the right one for me'" (Judges 14:3). God isn't against interracial marriages; the race doesn't matter to God. What God is concerned about is who people worship, who they call their God.

As you might have guessed, that marriage didn't last very long. You would think that Samson would have learned his lesson and never made that mistake again, but he's a lot like us! The next woman he fell for was a Philistine named Delilah. Rather than learning from his past mistakes and following God's guidelines, Samson once again set himself up for heartache by getting entangled with a nonbeliever and falling in love.

Delilah didn't have Samson's interests at heart. She wasn't looking for true love and companionship. She didn't want to make a marriage commitment. She just wanted to set him up so that she would receive a reward from the Philistines. As sad as it may seem, some people just want to set you up. Sometimes people just want to have the bragging rights of saying they slept with someone.

LOVE LESSONS

Why should we avoid dating a non-Christian?

What did you learn from Samson's life about dating? What specifically would you avoid?

How can an unplanned date be dangerous?

THE LIE TO REJECT

I renounce the lie of Satan that I can be careless with my dating and not get hurt.

THE TRUTH TO ACCEPT

I accept the truth that God's guidelines for dating are best for me.

PRAYER FOR TODAY

Dear heavenly Father, I don't want to be like Samson and seek a relationship that's not from You. I choose to follow Your Word and not be careless with my heart. I choose to hide Your Word in my heart that I might not sin against You. Lord, the world around me looks like it's having so much fun. Please give me the wisdom to see the truth about false relationships and dating non-Christians. In Jesus' name I pray. Amen.

TODAY'S BIBLE READING

Proverbs 14:1-35
Theme: Good versus evil: round five

DAY TWENTY-FOUR

TREAT THEM RIGHT

A man's ways are in full view of the LORD, and he examines all his paths (Proverbs 5:21).

Dating is a serious responsibility. God expects you to treat the people you date the same way Jesus would treat them. Guys, you need to respect each girl and treat her the way you would want another guy to treat your future wife. Proverbs 5:21 says, "For a man's ways are in full view of the LORD, and he examines all his paths."

The time will come when you fall in love and your husband or wife to be will ask you, "Have you ever, you know, had sex with anyone else?" You will either be able to look him or her right in the eyes and say, "No, I waited for you" or your eyes will hit the floor and you'll have answered the question already!

The question will come. If you don't ask it, the other person will. A great deal of your strength depends on how you date. If you set up the right dating standards, it's a lot easier to maintain your purity. If you have poor dating habits, you're headed for a fall!

Most of us think of the dream date as involving the perfect person. That certainly can be part of it, but a good date should also have specified boundaries, be well-planned, and have a specific destination.

By the time I (Dave) entered college I had finally figured out that it was no fun to date unless I knew the other

129

person well. I had survived enough of those horrible dates where you both stare at each other not knowing what to say because you don't have a clue who the other person is. Boundaries are usually perceived as a negative: "Who wants boundaries? I want freedom!" Well, God doesn't give us boundaries to imprison us but to ensure our safety. He wants to *guard* us from evil and to *guide* us to His perfect will.

Boundary number one: Date people you know well. When my wife, Grace, and I first started to date it was easy because we had been good friends for quite some time before Grace looked at me one day and asked "Hey, are we dating?" "I guess we are," I replied. One of the first boundaries you need to make is that you won't date anyone you don't know well. Blind dates or last-minute dates are just invitations to trouble. Who you date is serious; we've heard too many horrible accounts of date rape and molestation. *Don't date anyone you don't know well—it's just not safe.*

Boundary number two: Go on a planned date. A *planned date* ensures you that you don't accidentally find yourself parked in the woods, out of gas, in temptation's trap. Ask the person you're dating where you're going. If there isn't a plan, then don't go. If the plan sounds like an invitation to trouble, then pass on the date. You need to avoid tempting situations. Romans 13:14 reminds us to "put on the Lord Jesus Christ and make no provision for the flesh in regard to its lusts" (NASB).

Only go to *safe places* where you're sure you won't be tempted sexually and you know you're protected from any possibility of date rape. *Group dating* with other believers is a good idea because it ensures your safety and testimony. What we're really talking about here is *accountability*. Ecclesiastes 4:9,10 says, "Two are better than one, because they have a good return for their work: If one falls down, his friend can help him up. But pity the man who falls and has no one to help him up!"

Boundary number three: Date strong believers. You want to date someone who has *God's interests at heart* and not his hormones. Nonbelievers can only imitate a walk in the Spirit, but a true believer who is strong in the Lord is more likely to help you avoid sexual temptation. Galatians 5:16 tells, "Walk by the Spirit and you will not carry out the desire of the flesh" (NASB). When you date a strong believer, sexual temptation doesn't stop. All of us can still be tempted, accused, and deceived, but you are more likely to spot the enemy's plans and submit yourselves to God for help. "Therefore encourage one another and build each other up, just as in fact you are doing" (1 Thessalonians 5:11).

Boundary number four: Pray and read God's word together. Right now you may be saying to yourself, "Pray? On a date? Are you crazy?" We know most couples don't pray when they go out together, but why shouldn't they? Ask yourself whether you want just a superficial relationship or whether you really want to know this person intimately. *Nothing lets you know a person's heart for God like prayer.* God also promised that He would draw near to us when we take the time to draw near to Him (James 4:8).

What's the whole purpose of dating, anyway? Yes, it's to get to know the other person well, but it's also to grow closer to God as a couple. If the second part of that sentence is missing in your relationship, then true intimacy isn't possible. We draw closer to God and to each other by being in His Word together as well. Jeremiah 15:16 says, "When your words came, I ate them; they were my joy and my heart's delight, for I bear your name, O LORD God Almighty." Who doesn't want joy and delight in his or her dating life?

Boundary number five: Be a living testimony together. Hebrews 12:2 tells us to "fix our eyes on Jesus, the author and perfecter of our faith, who for the joy set before him endured the cross, scorning its shame, and sat down at the right hand of the throne of God." Fixing our eyes on Jesus is relatively easy at church or youth group gatherings, but what happens when you're away from church and familiar Christian surroundings? Are you a good testimony of what you profess to believe? In other words, do people still see Christ in you?

Every date should have a spiritual side to it because you're a spiritual being. God is always with you. He indwells you, so you should always have a sense of His presence. If the person you're dating is two-faced, acting one way at church but then acting like hell on wheels everywhere else, he or she is showing you a real lack of spiritual maturity. Don't be afraid to let him or her go. The only thing you're losing is a heartache.

LOVE LESSONS

What boundaries do you currently have in your dating life? Take some time and list them!

What do you think is the most important boundary of all? Why?

What do you think happens to believers who date but have no boundaries at all? Have you seen any of your friends hurt that way?

Do you know what your date boundaries are? Have you ever talked about it?

THE LIE TO REJECT

I renounce the lie of Satan that I am unable to walk in the Spirit and control my dating life.

THE TRUTH TO ACCEPT

I accept the truth that God has empowered me with His Spirit and that I am able to live and date in a way that is pleasing to God.

PRAYER FOR TODAY

Dear heavenly Father, I know that my ways are in Your full view. I want my life to please You in every way. I choose to walk in the Spirit and not carry out the desires of the flesh. I want to be prepared to stand against any temptation. I choose to make clear boundaries that I can follow. I know that You supply all the strength I need to walk in Your ways. In Jesus' name I pray. Amen.

TODAY'S BIBLE READING

Proverbs 15:1-33
Theme: Good versus evil: round six

Fix Your Eyes

Let us fix our eyes on Jesus, the author and perfecter of our faith, who for the joy set before him endured the cross, scorning its shame, and sat down at the right hand of the throne of God (Hebrews 12:2).

Maybe you're presently involved in a bad dating relationship. You know it's not from God. His Word shows you this, but your heart and feelings are telling you to hold on because this might be true love. "Okay," you say to yourself, "I know he doesn't know Christ personally but I'm sure it'll work out!"

Or maybe you're afraid that this is your one and only chance at love. But if you have to compromise God's Word or your purity, it's not love. You're being deceived; Satan is trying to trick you so you'll miss God's best for you. God's Word gives us guidelines not to hurt us but to help us. *God is love,* so He always wants the best for you. *God is all-powerful,* so He can bring the right people into your life. *God is all-knowing,* so He knows just how to show you who that special person is for you.

If you sense that you're involved in a relationship that might compromise your purity, then end that relationship now! Remember, God created you for a love relationship with Himself. Nurture your relationship with God first and then all the other important relationships will fall into place. "Let us fix our eyes on Jesus, the author and perfecter of our faith, who for the joy set before him endured the cross, scorning its shame, and sat down at the right hand of the throne of God" (Hebrews 12:2).

One girl wrote this letter to me after attending a *Stomping Out the Darkness* conference. She shared with me a painful but powerful lesson.

Dear Dave,

I just wanted you to know that Jesus has been speaking through you this week and that lives (I'm sure more than mine) have been touched and changed. This week I've forgiven my father for hurting me—something that has taken years. And I did forgive him: I broke down in tears in the middle of the evening session; I was so glad I didn't wait until I *felt* like forgiving him.

Dave, I know my life has been changed this week. Last year at this time I was engaged to be married. I am no longer engaged. I loved him very much, but he broke off the relationship. He gave me no explanation, except that he chose to give everything to his future career.

I dealt with the breakup okay for about four months, until I learned that while he was engaged to me he had another girlfriend. My anger began to get out of control. You see, during our relationship we also had a sexual relationship. While we never went all the way, we had come so far and so close, that actual sex was all that was left. I allowed him to touch and kiss me, and do things with me I never even knew were possible. My whole reasoning for my behavior was "I'm going to marry him anyhow, so what does it matter?" Talk about deception!

While I know now that he was not God's choice for my husband, I also know that God has a perfect guy out there for me. I know that I sinned, but because I renounced that sin and asked for God's forgiveness, I am pure in the eyes of God. Dave, thanks for your dedication to the Lord and to your ministry.

Love in Christ,
Anna

Love Lessons

It's important now that you take some time and ask God to reveal to you any of Satan's evil lies about your dating life and relationships.

Have you ever been tempted to compromise your purity or commitment for the Lord because of a relationship you have had? Explain.

What did you think about Anna when you read her letter? What did you think of her old fiancé?

What would you share with a friend who was struggling to end a bad relationship?

The Lie to Reject

I renounce the lie of Satan that I can compromise my purity, go outside of God's loving guidelines, and still find peace.

The Truth to Accept

I accept the truth that God knows what is best for me and gives me guidelines because He loves me and wants to protect me.

PRAYER FOR TODAY

Dear Lord, I ask You to reveal to my mind if I have the right attitude when it comes to dating. I want to keep my ways pure and follow Your Word (Psalm 119:11). I choose to fix my eyes on Jesus and His ways (Hebrews 12:2). I believe that Your Word is the only reliable guide for my dating life. I have trusted Jesus to save me, so I know I'm His child. Therefore, by the authority of the Lord Jesus Christ I command all evil spirits to leave my presence. I ask You, Lord, to look deep inside me and reveal to me my true attitudes and actions. In Jesus' name I pray. Amen.

TODAY'S BIBLE READING

Proverbs 16:1-33
Theme: Godly living: part one

Part Six

Love and Sex

BUILT-IN CONSEQUENCES

Marriage should be honored by all, and the marriage bed kept pure, for God will judge the adulterer and all the sexually immoral (Hebrews 13:4).

Everything we do and every choice we make has built-in consequences.

In early 1988 Charles and Diana, Prince and Princess of Wales, and some friends took a skiing trip to Switzerland. The shocking news came one afternoon of a terrible accident caused by an avalanche in which one of the prince's lifelong friends was killed and another was seriously injured. It seemed sheer chance that the Prince himself was not killed or hurt.

How did it happen? A day or two later the press reported that the Prince's group had chosen to ski out on slopes that were closed to the public. The avalanche warnings had been posted, but [the group] had chosen to go beyond the fence because, as one of them observed, that is where the optimum fun and excitement were to be found. Most likely they found a branch of pleasure that was indeed more than attractive. But it went beyond the margins of what was safe and wise. And the avalanche made them pay a price for who went beyond the fences.

The result? Several broken worlds. Like the Prince and his party who could not stay inside the fences, all of us become curious enough at times to edge out to the fences

141

and see what is on the on the other side. Perhaps we become curious to see how far we can sneak away from God and not suffer the consequences.[1]

The same is true of our response to God's plan for sex and marriage. If we stay within the boundaries of sexual purity in our relationships and marriages, we will reap the benefits and blessings. Paul said it this way: "The one who sows to his own flesh shall from the flesh reap corruption, but the one who sows to the Spirit shall from the Spirit reap eternal life" (Galatians 6:8 NASB).

As I (Dave) traveled with Josh McDowell it was the beginning of a sexual purity campaign called "Why Wait." Time and time again I heard Josh say, "Within every negative commandment are two positive principles. God wants to *protect* something and God wants to *provide* for something."

Like Charles and Diana, you may see the signs that say "Do not enter" and think they are there to restrict your fun. But in reality they are there to protect you from harm and lead you to the places where the safest and best fun can be had. Charles and Di may be royalty, but they still have to follow the same protective guidelines that govern you and me. And while it's true that you are a child of the Most High God, if you step outside of God's protective commandments, an avalanche of sinful consequences will soon bury and smother your spiritual life and sometimes your physical life as well.

Perhaps the most alarming fallout from ignoring God's design for sex is the physical consequences. Physical pain, the threat of disease and death, get our attention quickly.

Free sex isn't free, and those who pursue it aren't living in freedom. Sexual promiscuity leads to disgusting forms of bondage, and the potential price tag in terms of health is staggering. Dr. Joe McIlhaney, a gynecologist, states that 30 percent of single, sexually active Americans have herpes. Another 30 percent have venereal wart virus. As many as 30 to 40 percent have chlamydia, which is rampant among teenagers and college students. Cases of gonorrhea and syphilis are increasing at an alarming rate.[2] Medical health experts insist that sexually transmitted diseases (STD's) are by far the most prevalent of communicable diseases.

The most frightening aspect of STD's is that they can be passed on without the carrier exhibiting any symptoms. This is especially true for those who test positive for HIV. Victims may go for years without showing signs of illness, unknowingly passing on the disease to their sexual partners, who in turn pass it on to other unsuspecting victims. Without medical testing, a person cannot be sure that his or her sexual partner is free of all STD's. Indeed, the partner may not even know that he himself is infected.

The rapid spread of STD's in our culture illustrates the chilling truth that a sexual encounter involves more than two people. If you have sex with a promiscuous person, as far as STD's are concerned, you are also having sex with every one of that person's previous sex partners, and you are vulnerable to the diseases carried by all of them.

LOVE LESSONS

Why does God give us boundaries in our lives?

Why do you think sexual purity is such a big deal to God?

When God said we shouldn't be involved sexually before marriage, what does He want to protect us from?

What does God want to provide for us by helping us to be sexually pure?

The Lie to Reject

I renounce the lie of Satan that I can compromise my sexual purity and not have any consequences.

The Truth to Accept

I accept the truth that God gives me loving guidelines because He wants to protect me and provide the best foundation for a solid relationship with my future mate.

Prayer for Today

Dear Heavenly Father, I thank You that Your Word shoots straight with me. At times, I admit, I don't like the commands in Your Word because they sound negative and restricting. I want my freedom, but I realize that You know what's best for me. I know that Your commands were given to protect me and to provide true freedom for me. I choose to obey Your Word and hold marriage in an honored place in my heart. I choose to keep the marriage bed pure; I don't want to have to bear the consequence of sin. In Jesus' name I pray. Amen.

Today's Bible Reading

Proverbs 17:1-28
Theme: Godly living: part two

Day Twenty-Seven

Think About the Future

Each of you should learn to control his own body in a way that is holy and honorable, not in passionate lust like the heathen, who do not know God (I Thessalonians 4:4,5).

Teenagers who have violated God's design for sex also pay a price in their future marriage relationships. Those who have had unholy sex don't seem to enjoy holy sex. We have counseled many women who can't stand to be touched by their husbands due to past illicit sexual experiences. Incredibly, their feelings change almost immediately after finding their freedom in Christ from sexual bondages.

Your mind is a powerful tool. It can store and recall an incredible amount of information. If you're involved sexually before marriage or outside of marriage, those memories can come back to haunt you. No one wants to be compared to another sex partner. Those reruns in the mind give the enemy ammunition to use against you. That type of accusation can't happen if he has nothing to draw from.

Sex before marriage seems to lead to lack of sexual fulfillment after marriage. The fun and excitement of sex outside God's will leaves the participant in bondage to illicit encounters and unable to enjoy a normal sexual relationship.

In every relationship there will come a time when your husband or wife will ask you about your sexual past. If your life has been filled with sexual exploits your mate will more than likely struggle with trusting you. Every relationship needs trust. In fact, our relationship with Christ is based on trusting Him and understanding how dependable He is. Trust can be rebuilt in time, but it's much easier to simply to keep your slate clean in the first place.

Another relationship issue is your virginity. You can give it away only once. While traveling with Josh I heard him tell the story of a girl who was determined to save herself for her husband. Every day at school her girlfriends would tease her and tell her that she wasn't a woman if she hadn't had sex yet. They would brag about the sex they had had with their boyfriends.

Finally, after she had had enough of their bragging, she replied, "Anytime I want to I can become like you, but you can never again become like me!" That girl knew she could give away her virginity only once.

God doesn't want sex to be the dominant reason you're together as a couple. He wants you to know the difference between true love and sex. If you're sexually involved with another person before marriage, your mind is focusing on getting sex and not on developing the other person and the relationship.

The biggest relationship issue of all is with God. Sexual sin cuts off God's ability to bless you and lead you to the deep love and freedom that can be found only in a pure relationship. Sexual sin makes God move into the area of discipline. God wants to protect your testimony so you will always be able to witness and share the love of Christ with others.

Often we are asked, "How far can I go physically and not get in trouble?" The question really needs some adjustment: "How can I nurture purity?" Still, what about holding hands, kissing, French kissing, or exploring someone's body and sex? By now you have a fairly good idea what God would have to say about some of these areas.

Let's imagine for a moment that Jesus could have dated and gotten married. Now we know that this wasn't His purpose; He came to save us from our sins and give us eternal life. But if He had dated, what would He have done on a date? When would He have held hands, kissed, or more? Take a minute and put an "X" in the list below at the point you think Jesus would have done these things.

WHAT WOULD JESUS DO?				
First Date	**Steady**	**Promised**	**Engaged**	**Married**

Do you know what you just did? You made rules for a holy God. You told Him when you thought it was right for Him to hold hands, kiss, and so on. Let me ask you this: Do you think your rules or guidelines will be stricter or more lenient than God's? Most young people we ask that question say that God's rules will be stricter.

Almost every young Christian we have fill out the chart is really tough on Jesus. We know sex and exploring must be saved for marriage, but some youth won't even let Jesus hold hands until He's married. The point is that if you follow

God's guidelines in His Word and your own convictions for Jesus, you probably won't get into too much trouble. Try out the chart on others. See what they do with Jesus. Does your chart match theirs, and most important of all, does it match up with God's Word?

God wants to provide you with the very best marriage and only good memories. What some people call freedom is really bondage, so be careful. If there is even a question in your mind about what you are doing—stop. A life filled with guilt and bondage is not meant for you!

LOVE LESSONS

Take some time to write out what you would do on a date.

Why do you think it's important to set dating guidelines before you actually date?

What did you think about the girl who was teased by her friends? Have you ever had to make that kind of stand? Are you willing to?

What are some of the bad effects of sex before marriage?

What are some of the positive benefits of waiting until you're married before you're sexually involved?

THE LIE TO REJECT

I renounce the lie of Satan that I can't control my body and say no to sex before marriage.

The Truth to Accept

I accept the truth that God never asks me to do anything that is impossible for me to do. So I choose to control my body and save sex until my wedding night.

Prayer for Today

Dear heavenly Father, I know that You want to give me the very best marriage and only good memories. I choose to turn away from a life filled with guilt and bondage, and turn to You and Your ways. I choose to set guidelines in my dating life, and by the power of Your Spirit I choose to control my body. I choose to save the sexual use of my body for my future mate so that my wedding night will be a special gift for him or her. In Jesus' name I pray. Amen.

Today's Bible Reading

Proverbs 18:1-24
Theme: Godly living: part three

YOU ARE NOT YOUR OWN

Do you not know that your body is a temple of the Holy Spirit, who is in you, whom you have received from God? You are not your own; you were bought at a price. Therefore honor God with your body (1 Corinthians 6:19-20).

Many young people find that their uncontrolled sexual desires lead them into physical relationships and even deeper bondage. Many head down the path of sexual experimentation believing that they will never get pulled in too far. Some rationalize, "I'm not actually having sex, so no harm is done, right?" Wrong! Fondling and exploring another person's body can cause you to lose your freedom.

We must understand how God views us and our bodies. You are not a plaything to be used to satisfy someone's sex drive. You are a temple of the Holy Spirit. First Corinthians 6:19,20 says, "Do you not know that your body is a temple of the Holy Spirit, who is in you, whom you have received from God? You are not your own; you were bought at a price. Therefore honor God with your body."

When the Bible says that you are a temple of the Holy Spirit it refers to you as the holy of holies, the *naos*. That term referred to the place where only God dwelt. Only once a year was a high priest from the tribe of Levi allowed to enter. Then if he had even a single sin in his life that was undealt with, he died!

When you accepted Christ you became God's holy of holies, a place where God dwells in His fullness and holiness. With that in mind, is sexual exploration of a Christian's body a big deal to God? You bet it is! First Thessalonians 4:4,5 reminds us that "each of you should learn to control his own body in a way that is holy and honorable, not in passionate lust like the heathen, who do not know God."

Sexual exploration steals the sexual joy that will come later in marriage. No one wants to have to explain to her future husband how she let a half-dozen other people touch her body. A person who opens the door to fondling is responding to lust, not love. He or she is only seeking immediate pleasure. He's not thinking about the future and the one he should save his body for. When a relationship becomes sexual, you don't have on your mind how to love and nurture the other person. Your mind is now preoccupied with sexual desire.

Maybe you've read the book *The Lion, The Witch and the Wardrobe*. In chapter 3, Edmund finds his way into the land of Narnia and meets the terrible white witch. When she finds out that he is a human and from the outside world, she tempts him to bring his brother and sisters to her with Turkish Delight.

> At last the Turkish Delight was all finished and Edmund was looking very hard at the empty box and wishing that she would ask him whether he would like some more. Probably the Queen knew quite well what he was thinking; for she knew, though Edmund did not, that this was enchanted Turkish Delight and that anyone who had once tasted it would want more and more of it, and would even, if they were allowed, go eating until they killed themselves.[3]

You know where we're going with this story, don't you? Touching where you shouldn't touch leads to more touching. First Peter 2:11 tells us, "Dear friends, I urge you, as aliens and strangers in the world, to abstain from sinful desires, which war against your soul." "Abstain" means don't go near, keep away from it, don't touch it. Inappropriate touch is like Turkish Delight—you just want more and more. Where does the cycle begin? With an unplanned date, not determining ahead of time what your boundaries are going to be. When a tempting sexual thought comes into your mind, tell it to get out!

Also be sure to watch out for the pressure lines, such as: "If you love me you'll let me." Whenever you hear a pressure line it means it's not true love. True love never pressures. In fact, Jesus doesn't even pressure people to accept Him as Savior, because when you're pressuring someone it's never done in love. If you're being pressured sexually you may want to reconsider the relationship. Remember Samson? The pressure from Delilah finally got the best of him. And it cost him a lot—his freedom and eventually his life. Don't play with fire, get out of the tempting situation immediately.

Love Lessons

What does the Bible mean when it says we are a temple of the Holy Spirit? How does the fact that you're God's temple make you feel?

How do we honor God with our bodies?

How can uncontrolled sexual desires lead to even deeper bondage?

If your relationship is built on just sexual desire, what are you missing or leaving out?

Have you ever been pressured sexually? What are some of the pressure lines you've heard?

THE LIE TO REJECT

I renounce the lie of Satan that my body is my own to do with as I please.

THE TRUTH TO ACCEPT

I accept the truth that my body belongs to God because I am His child, and that my body is to be a special gift for my mate.

PRAYER FOR TODAY

Dear Heavenly Father, I know that my body is a temple of the Holy Spirit and that You live in me. Your presence in my life is a special gift from You. I know that my body is not just my own but it belongs to You and my future mate after marriage. So because I am Your child I choose to honor You with my body. In Jesus' name I pray. Amen.

TODAY'S BIBLE READING

Proverbs 19:1-29
Theme: Godly living: part four

It's Not Just You

There is nothing concealed that will not be disclosed, or hidden that will not be made known (Matthew 10:26).

Sexual sin affects you and your family. The affair between King David of Israel and Bathsheba, wife of Uriah, gives us a sad example of what can happen when you ignore God's guidelines. Even though David was called a man after God's own heart (Acts 13:22), he had one dark blot on his life. First Kings 15:5 summarizes his life: "David had done what was right in the eyes of the Lord and had not failed to keep any of the Lord's commands all the days of his life—except in the case of Uriah the Hittite." And because of his moral failure, David's family paid a steep price. Let's take a look at his fatal steps and their tragic consequences.

"One evening David got up from his bed and walked around on the roof of the palace. From the roof he saw a woman bathing. The woman was very beautiful, and David sent someone to find out about her" (2 Samuel 11:2,3). There was nothing wrong with Bathsheba being beautiful, and there was nothing wrong with David being attracted to her. That's the way God made us. We might say, "Hey, girl, didn't anybody ever tell you not to take a bath where people can see you?" So Bathsheba may have been wrong for bathing where others could see her, and David was definitely wrong for continuing to look at her. God provided a way of escape: David could have turned and walked away from the tempting sight. But he didn't take the escape route.

When David sent messengers to get Bathsheba, he was too far down the path of immorality to turn around. They slept together, and she became pregnant. David tried to cover up his sin by calling Uriah, Bathsheba's husband, home from the battlefield to sleep with her. The pregnancy could then be attributed to him. But Uriah wouldn't cooperate, so David sent him back to the battle and arranged for him to be killed. Now David was not only an adulterer but also a murderer! Sin has a way of compounding itself. If you think living righteously is hard, try living unrighteously. Cover-up, denial, and guilt make for a very complex life. You have to remember who you lied to and what you said.

After a period of mourning her dead husband, Bathsheba became David's wife. David lived under the guilt and covered his shame for nine months. He apparently suffered physical consequences because of his sin. In Psalm 32:3 he describes his torment: "When I kept silent, my bones wasted away through my groaning all day long. For day and night your hand was heavy upon me; my strength was sapped as in the heat of summer."

David's troubles remind us of an old D.L. Moody story we came across in the Gordon McDonald book *Rebuilding Your Broken World*. Moody writes:

> Dr. Andrew Bonar told me how, in the Highlands of Scotland, sheep would often wander off into the rocks and get into places that they couldn't get out of. The grass on these mountains is very sweet and the sheep like it, and they will jump down ten or twelve feet, and then they can't jump back again and the shepherd hears them bleating in distress. They may be there for days, until they have eaten all the grass. The shepherd will wait until they are so faint that they cannot stand, and

then they will put a rope around them, and he will go over and pull the sheep up out of the jaws of death.

"Why don't they go down there when the sheep first get there?" I asked.

"Ah," he said, "they are so very foolish they would dash right over the precipice and be killed if they did."

Moody concludes his story by saying:

And that is the way with men: They won't go back to God till they have no friends and have lost everything. If you are a wanderer I tell you that the Good Shepherd will bring you back the moment you have given up trying to save yourself and are willing to let Him save you His own way.[4]

The Lord allowed plenty of time for David to come to terms with his sin. The king didn't confess, so God sent the prophet Nathan to confront him. God won't let His children live in darkness for long, because He knows it will eat them alive. One pastor with a pornography addiction traveled to a pastor's conference, where colleagues asked for copies of his ministry materials. When the pastor opened the briefcase with a crowd around him, he suddenly realized he had brought the wrong case. His stack of smutty magazines was there for all to see!

"There is nothing concealed that will not be disclosed, or hidden that will not be made known" (Matthew 10:26).

Love Lessons

What other sins did David's uncontrolled sexual desire lead to?

List all the people you can think of who were affected by David's sin.

How was David affected physically and spiritually by his sin?

Why do you think the Bible still says David was a man after God's own heart even though he committed such terrible sins?

The Lie to Reject

I renounce the lie of Satan that I can hide my sin or that my sin doesn't hurt others.

The Truth to Accept

I accept the truth that God sees all that I do. I know my sins will be exposed, so I choose to repent quickly and follow the Lord.

Prayer for Today

Dear Lord, I know at times I try to hide my sin, but You see all my deeds and still love me. I choose to keep my heart soft and repent of my sins by turning away quickly from my sinful ways. Lord, I want to follow You. I don't want my sin to hurt others. Most of all I don't want to disappoint You. I want to experience Your blessings, not Your discipline. Lord, show me if I'm hiding any sin because I want to be right with You. In Jesus' name I pray. Amen.

Today's Bible Reading

Proverbs 20:1-30
Theme: Godly living: part five

BREAKING THE CHAINS

He who conceals his sins does not prosper, but whoever confesses and renounces them finds mercy (Proverbs 28:13).

Repentance is God's answer to sin and self-reliance. To repent means to have a change of mind about sin and to renounce it. Repentance is far more than just saying what I did was wrong, however. It means to turn from our self-centered ways and trust in God. It means to no longer hold iniquity or rebellion in our hearts. We commit all we have and all we are to God. In this way we are being faithful stewards of everything God has entrusted to us (1 Corinthians 4:1,2).

Such a commitment should include our possessions, our ministries, our families, and the activity of our physical bodies, including sexual activity. As we renounce any previous use of these for the service of sin and then dedicate them to the Lord, we are saying that the god of this world no longer has any right over them. They now belong to God, and Satan can't have them or use them.

God forgives us when we repent, but He doesn't necessarily take away all the consequences of our sin. If He did, it wouldn't take us long to figure out that we can sin all we want and then turn to God for cleansing without any consequences.

Also remember that bad health can be contagious but good health isn't. Paul wrote, "Do not be misled: 'Bad company corrupts good character'" (1 Corinthians 15:33).

David's sexual sin and murderous cover-up were tragic, and the consequences of sin in his own life and in the lives of his children were painful and long-lasting. But his story has a happy ending. David responded to his sin correctly and went on to shepherd Israel with integrity of heart and lead them with skillful hands (Psalm 78:72). And from him came the Messiah, who promised to save us from our sin (Genesis 3:15).

David's confession of sin in Psalm 51 is a model prayer for those who violate God's plan for sex:

> Have mercy on me, O God, according to your unfailing love; according to your great compassion blot out my transgressions. Wash away all my iniquity and cleanse me from my sin. For I know my transgressions, and my sin is always before me. Against you, you only, have I sinned and done what is evil in your sight, so that you are proved right when you speak and justified when you judge....
>
> Create in me a pure heart, O God, and renew a steadfast spirit within me. Do not cast me from your presence or take your Holy Spirit from me. Restore to me the joy of your salvation and grant me a willing spirit, to sustain me (verses 1-4, 10-12).

But what if we sin and don't confess? What if we get caught up in pornography, lust, sexual fantasy, or affairs, and keep it a secret instead of exposing it to the light? What kind of consequences can we expect?

In addition to the physical and relational consequences, continued sexual sin leads us down a dark path to the dead end of sexual bondage.

LOVE LESSONS

What does repentance mean?

How is repentance different from just saying I'm sorry for my sin?

What happens if we sin but don't confess and renounce our sin?

Have you seen the bad effects of sin around you? Are there specific people you know who suffer from such effects?

THE LIE TO REJECT

I renounce the lie that I can find mercy apart from turning from my sin.

THE TRUTH TO ACCEPT

I accept the truth that God gives me mercy when I confess and renounce my sin and follow God's ways.

PRAYER FOR TODAY

Dear Lord, I ask You to reveal to my mind if I have anything I need to renounce, because I want to be clean in Your eyes. I choose not to hide my sin but to ask You to reveal to me any way that I might have broken Your holy law. I know that Christ's death paid the penalty for my sin so I'm forgiven, but I don't want to use my body as an instrument of unrighteousness. Rather, I choose to

*present my body to You as a living and holy sacrifice. In
Jesus' name I pray. Amen.*

TODAY'S BIBLE READING

Proverbs 21:1-31
Theme: Godly living: part six

PART SEVEN

Love and the Second Chance

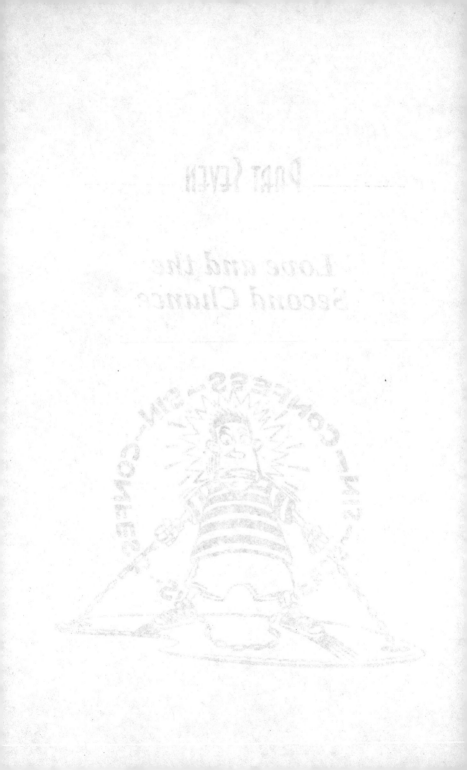

Second Chance

*If we walk in the light, as he is in the light, we have
fellowship with one another, and the blood of Jesus,
his Son, purifies us from all sin. If we claim to be
without sin, we deceive ourselves and the truth is not
in us. If we confess our sins, he is faithful and just
and will forgive us our sins and purify us from all
unrighteousness* (1 John 1:7-9).

There is no doubt that God wants us to escape the
heartache and pain of sexual sin. But what if you have
already blown it sexually?

"I know God will forgive me," you may say.

The real question most people struggle with is "Will
God ever use me? Will I get a second chance? Will my life
count for God?"

Check out this story. Read it carefully because it's not
made up. It's real!

> Until I was 29, I longed to be held in the arms of a man.
> I wanted security, and I thought it was to be found in a
> man who would draw me to himself, lay my head on
> his chest, and become my protector, my sustainer for
> life. To me this was the epitome of life. It was all I
> wanted.
>
> I didn't find it in my first husband. On the second day
> of our honeymoon, my husband—my capable, talented,
> athletic husband—went into depression. Instead of

being loving and protecting, Tom began to tell me all the things he didn't like about me and that he wanted changed. That was just the beginning of the ups and downs of his mood swings. Some days were wonderful. On those days I loved keeping his house, entertaining his friends, and being his wife. But when he would become depressed, my protector was gone and I would fight for survival. I was determined not to be destroyed.

We went to church. We knew the name "God." We knew His Son's name, Jesus. We bore His name, "Christian." But we really didn't know *Him*. We thought we did. We never heard or saw anything that would make us question whether we were Christians. But then if we knew any real Christians, I was not aware of it. We were all the same. We played church.

Finally I couldn't handle the depression anymore. I was too self-centered. I left Tom and took our sons, Tommy and Mark, with me. Yet the longing for security remained. I wanted to be held. I wanted to be loved just as I was, no strings attached—loved whether I was pretty or ugly, sick or well, in a good mood or a bad mood. I wanted to be loved regardless of what I was like. I wanted to be loved unconditionally.

I began my search. I went from one man to another. In the process I became something I never wanted, never dreamed I would ever be. I became an adulteress. Yet all I wanted was security.

When I was 29, my search ended on my knees beside my bed, for there I met my El Shaddai. . . . Time and time again I have found Him to be my all-sufficient God, my protector, the unconditional lover of my soul. He held me through the suicide of my first husband. He held me as a single parent when at times I was over-whelmed by loneliness, responsibility, and the need to be held. He has held me though times of great financial need, both personally and in our ministry. He has held me when the pains of leadership have seemed almost overwhelming. He has held me when I have failed. He has held me when I have cried for my children and poured out my doubts about being a good mother.[1]

Could God ever use that person? Her name is Kay Arthur. Kay is a best-selling author, and her Bible study methods are being used all over the world. Kay knows who she is in Christ and can walk free from her past because she is a new creature in Christ.

The miracle is that Jesus gives that opportunity to experience new life and freedom to everyone. Yes, God is the God of the second chance. He wants to use *you*. He wants *your* life to be a shining example to everyone around you of what God can do!

Love Lessons

How do we walk in the light with our sin? What happens if we don't?

Why does God ask us to confess our sin to Him? Doesn't He know about our sin already?

What about Kay's story touched you the most? Write down how you felt after you found out who this person was.

Have you ever felt like God would never use you because of a sin in your past? Why would Satan want you to believe that God would never use a person with a dark past?

THE LIE TO REJECT

I renounce the lie of Satan that my past sexual sin determines who I am or how I can be used by God.

THE TRUTH TO ACCEPT

I accept the truth that God has forgiven me of all my sins and that I am now a new creature in Christ, my past is forgiven, and everything has been made brand-new.

PRAYER FOR TODAY

Dear Lord, thank You for being the God of the second chance. I choose to confess and renounce the sin You reveal to my mind. I want to be pure in Your eyes. More than being forgiven of all my sins, I want to be used by You to reach others with the good news of Jesus. I know that there are so many people around me that are trapped in their sins. Lord, I want You to use me to show them the way to Jesus. In Jesus' name I pray. Amen.

TODAY'S BIBLE READING

Proverbs 22:1-16
Theme: Godly living: part seven

GIVE YOUR BOD TO GOD!

Do not let sin reign in your mortal body so that you obey its evil desires. Do not offer the parts of your body to sin, as instruments of wickedness, but rather offer yourselves to God, as those who have been brought from death to life; and offer the parts of your body to him as instruments of righteousness (Romans 6:12,13).

For many young Christians in bondage to sexual sin, life is usually going through the sin-confess-sin-confess-sin-I-give-up cycle. Some go to summer camp and rededicate their lives to Christ, only to have their commitments fade by the time school starts. Others hear a powerful sermon and their lives are moved. They're on fire for the Lord, but only for a short time. Soon they go back to their old ways of thinking and believing.

Why does all this happen? Because too many young Christians identity with the first Adam—with the Adam who sinned. Those who have trusted Christ are no longer identified with Adam and his sin, but with Jesus and His righteousness. We are not locked outside God's presence, as Adam was. We are seated with Christ in the heavenly places. The difference between Adam and Christ is eternally profound.

Our spiritual relationship with God is complete and eternal because it is provided by Christ. The Christian life is not meant to be a few brief shots of freedom. Freedom is our birthright every day of our lives. When you were born spiritually, God wrote your name in Jesus' book of life (see Revelation 21:27) and you became a citizen of heaven. As long as Christ remains alive spiritually, we will remain alive spiritually—and that's forever. We must live by faith in accordance with the truth. The key thought is this: *It's not what you do that sets you free from sexual bondage, it's what you believe.*

However, according to Romans 6:12,13, there is also something we must do in response to what God has already done. But beware: What God calls you to do in verses 12 and 13 will not be effective in your life if you're not believing what God has called you to believe in verses 1-11. It is the *truth* that sets us free, and *believing the truth* must precede and determine responsible behavior.

Paul says, "Therefore do not let sin reign in your mortal body so that you obey its evil desires" (verse 12). According to this verse, whose job is it not to allow sin to reign in our bodies? Clearly it is ours as believers. This means we cannot say, "The devil made me do it." God never commands us to do something we cannot do or that the devil can prevent us from doing. In Christ you have died to sin, and the devil can't make you do anything. He will tempt you, accuse you, and try to deceive you. But if sin reigns in your body, it is because you allowed it to happen. You are responsible for your own attitudes and actions.

How then do we prevent sin from reigning in our bodies? Paul answers in verse 13: "Do not offer the parts of your body to sin, as instruments of wickedness, but rather offer yourselves to God, as those who have been brought from death to life; and offer the parts of your body to him as instruments of righteousness."

1. *Don't offer your body to sin.* We are not to use our eyes, hands, feet, etc. in any way that would serve sin. So when you're surfing the channel on TV and stop to watch the *Sports Illustrated* swimsuit special and linger lustfully to watch it, you are offering your body to sin. When you try to explore someone else's body, you are offering your body to sin. When you fantasize sexually about someone and act out your desires through masturbation, you are offering your body to sin. Whenever you choose to offer yourself to sin, you invite sin to rule in your physical body, something God has commanded you not to do.

2. *Offer yourself and your body to God.* Notice that Paul makes a distinction between "yourselves" and "the parts of your body." What is the distinction? Self is who we are on the inside—the immortal, outside part of us. Our bodies and their various parts are who we are on the outside—the mortal, temporary part of us. Someday we are going to get rid of these old earth suits. At that time we will be absent from our mortal bodies and present with the Lord in immortal bodies (2 Corinthians 5:8). As long as we are on planet Earth, however, our inner selves are united with our outer physical bodies. We are to offer the complete package—body, soul, and spirit—to God.

You have opportunities every day to offer your eyes, your hands, your brain, your feet, etc. to sin or to God. The Lord commands us to be good stewards of our bodies and to use them only as instruments of righteousness. But ultimately it's our own choice.

What happens when a child of God who is united with the Lord and one spirit with Him also misuses his or her body sexually with someone else? The Bible says he becomes one flesh with the object of his sin; they bond together. Bonding is a positive thing in a wholesome relationship, but in an immoral union bonding only leads to bondage.

How many times have you heard of a nice Christian girl who becomes involved with an immoral guy, has sex with him, and then continues in a sick relationship? He takes advantage of her and abuses her. Friends and relatives tell her, "He's no good for you." But she won't listen to them. Even though her boyfriend treats her badly, the girl won't leave him.

Why? Because a spiritual and emotional bond has formed. They have become one flesh. But such bonds must be broken. That's one reason why God instructs us not to become entangled with sexual activities and relationships in the first place.

This spiritual and emotional bond can occur even as a result of heavy sexual exploring.

Love Lessons

How then do we prevent sin from reigning in our bodies?

What happens when a child of God who is united with the Lord and one spirit with Him also misuses his or her body sexually with someone else?

Take some time now and offer your eyes, your hands, your brain, your feet, etc. to God.

The Lie to Reject

I renounce the lie of Satan that I have to live in bondage to my sins.

THE TRUTH TO ACCEPT

I accept the truth that God has set me free from my past and given me a new identity in Christ.

PRAYER FOR TODAY

Dear Lord, I know that You have set me free from my past through Christ's death on the cross. Lord, I don't want to let sin rule my life, so I choose to present my body to You as an instrument of righteousness, set apart for You. Thank You for cleaning me from all my sin and declaring me holy and pure in Your sight. In Jesus' name I pray. Amen.

TODAY'S BIBLE READING

Proverbs 23:1-35
Theme: Practices

RETHINK HOW YOU THINK

Do not conform any longer to the pattern of this world, but be transformed by the renewing of your mind. Then you will be able to test and approve what God's will is—his good, pleasing and perfect will (Romans 12:2).

Imagine that you have worked all through high school for the same boss—a cantankerous, unreasonable grouch. The man is known throughout the company for busting the employees and chewing them out royally for even the slightest suspicion of a mistake. You learned early during your employment to walk on eggshells around the old grouch and avoid him as much as possible. Every time he appears at your door you automatically cringe in fear, expecting to get blasted, even if he has only come to borrow a paper clip.

One day you arrive at work to learn that the boss has been suddenly fired. You are no longer under his authority, and your relationship with him has ended. Your new boss is a saint—mild-mannered, kind, considerate, affirming. He clearly has the best interests of his employees at heart. But how do you think you'll behave around him? Whenever you see your new boss coming down the hall, you start looking for a place to hide, just like you did around the old boss. Whenever the man comes up to you, your heart jumps into your throat. You wonder what you're going to get reamed out for this time. The more you get to know your new boss the more you realize he is as different from your old boss as night is from day. But it will take time to get to know your new boss and to change the negative reaction you learned under the old authority in your life.

Old habits are hard to break. Once we become programmed a certain way, it can be difficult to reprogram our minds. This is certainly true of established sexual thought patterns and habits which are contrary to God's Word, patterns which may have been ingrained in us long before we became Christians.

We are no longer under the authority of sin and Satan, because our relationship with them has been severed. We are new creations in Christ (2 Corinthians 5:17). But old thought patterns and habits of responding to temptations don't automatically go away; they are still with us. We have a new boss—Jesus Christ—but having lived under the domination of sin and Satan, we must adjust to the glorious freedom which our new boss has provided for us.

How does that happen? Paul called the process "renewing our minds." He urged, "Do not conform any longer to the pattern of this world, but be transformed by the renewing of your mind. Then you will be able to test and approve what God's will is—his good, pleasing and perfect will" (Romans 12:2). Next to what you believe about your relationship to sin, the two most critical issues you face in overcoming sexual bondage are presenting your physical body to God and renewing your mind to line up with God's truth.

Why is renewing the mind so critical? Because no one can consistently live in a way that is inconsistent with how he thinks or perceives himself. What we do doesn't determine who we are; who we are determines what we do. If you continue to think and respond as if you are under the dominion of your old boss, you will continue to live that way. You must change your thinking if you're going to change your behaving.

Why do we need to have our minds renewed? Before we placed our faith in Jesus Christ, we had neither the presence of God in our lives nor the knowledge of God's ways. So we learned how to live our lives independently of God and to gratify our sinful desires. We had no other choice.

Then one day we heard the gospel and decided to invite Jesus into our lives. We were born again. We became new creations in Christ. But unfortunately, there is no "erase" feature in this tremendous computer we call our mind. Everything that was previously programmed into our memory banks before we received Christ is still there. Our brains recorded every experience we ever had, good or bad. We remember all our sexual temptations and have stored away how good it felt to yield to them. If we don't reprogram our minds we will continue to respond to temptation the way we learned to under our old boss, Satan.

Because we are in Christ, "we have the mind of Christ" (1 Corinthians 2:16). We have superior weapons to win the battle for our minds.

LOVE LESSONS

Why do we need to have our minds renewed? Why is renewing the mind so critical to our success as Christians?

How do we go about renewing our minds?

What does renewing the mind destroy?

THE LIE TO REJECT

I renounce the lie of Satan that I chose to believe when I was under his authority.

THE TRUTH TO ACCEPT

I accept the truth that God has given me the Holy Spirit and I can have the mind of Christ.

PRAYER FOR TODAY

Dear Lord, I know that I was born into a sinful world and that I learned how to live independent of You. I know now, Lord, that I need to reject the lies and choose to believe the truth. I choose to renew my mind by spending time in Your Word, the Bible. I know that my faith will increase as well as my ability to say no to sin as I renew my mind with Your truth. Thank You that Your Word is truth and that I can trust in it. In Jesus' name I pray. Amen.

TODAY'S BIBLE READING

Proverbs 24:1-34
Theme: People

First-Frame Thinking

Though we live in the world, we do not wage war as the world does. The weapons we fight with are not the weapons of the world. On the contrary, they have divine power to demolish strongholds. We demolish arguments and every pretension that sets itself up against the knowledge of God, and we take captive every thought to make it obedient to Christ (2 Corinthians 10:3-5).

We must use God's weapons to change how we respond at the first frame of every sexual temptation. We must take those first thoughts captive and make them obedient to Christ. If we allow ourselves to continue thinking tempting thoughts, we will eventually act on them.

Suppose you struggle with lust. One night your mom asks you to go to the store for milk. When you get into the car, you wonder which store you should go to. You remember that the local convenience store has a display of pornographic magazines within easy reach. You can buy milk at other stores which don't sell those magazines, but the memory of the seductive photos you have ogled before at the convenience store gives rise to a tempting thought. The more you think about it, the harder it is to resist. When you pull out of the driveway, which way do you turn?

On the way to the convenience store, all kinds of thoughts cross your mind. You pray, "Lord, if You don't want me to look at the pornography, have my youth pastor be in the store buying milk or cause the store to be closed." Since the store is open (do you know any convenience stores that ever close?) and since the youth pastor isn't there, you decide it must be okay to take a look. The mind has an incredible way of rationalizing, which is why tempting thoughts must be stopped before your mind can come up with a reason to act on them.

But your stolen pleasure doesn't last. Before you leave the store, guilt and shame overwhelm you. "Why did I do it?" you moan. You did it primarily because you ignored the way of escape available to you before you even pulled out of the garage. *You failed to take that first thought captive and make it obedient to Christ.*

Why does our mind work this way? The Bible says that we have an outer self and an inner self (2 Corinthians 4:16). Our brain is part of the outer self. Our mind is a part of the inner self. There is something really different between our brain and our mind. Our brain is little more than meat. When we die physically our outer self, including our brain, will return to dust. Our inner self will be absent from the body and present with the Lord. We will be brainless, but we will not be mindless.

God has obviously created the outer self to go with the inner self. Our mind is the software. As the brain receives input, the mind compiles, analyzes, and interprets the data and chooses responses based on how the mind has been programmed. Before we came to Christ, our minds were programmed by the world, the flesh, and the devil, and our choices were made without the knowledge of God or the benefit of His presence. When we became Christians, nobody pressed the CLEAR button in our minds. We need to be reprogrammed by *God's truth.* We need our minds renewed, and this is the process of reprogramming the software.

How is our mind reprogrammed? Sexual behavior is usually the result of our thought life, and we do have control over what we think. If you fill your mind with pornography, your sex glands will begin to overreact and set in motion behavior that you will later regret.

One of the main ways we program our mind is through the eye-gate: what we see. Powerful things can happen in just seconds when we see something sexually explicit.

Have you ever wondered why it's so hard to remember some things and forget others? In school we study all night and then pray that the facts won't leave us before we take the big exam. But just one glance at a pornographic image seems to stay in our mind for years. Why is that?

When we are excited an autonomic signal is sent to the adrenal glands. A hormone called epinephrine goes into the bloodstream, which locks into our memory whatever picture is present at the time of the excitement. This reaction causes us to involuntarily remember events, whether bad or good. It's too bad we didn't get more excited with some of our subjects in school; we would have remembered them better!

LOVE LESSONS

Why is it so important to take a thought captive in the first frame?

Why do we remember some things and forget others?

How was our mind programmed before we came to Christ? How do we reprogram it?

THE LIE TO REJECT

I renounce the lie of Satan that I can let my mind think about sinful things and not sin.

THE TRUTH TO ACCEPT

I accept the truth that God has given me all the weapons I need to take every thought captive to the obedience of Christ.

PRAYER FOR TODAY

Dear Lord, I know that I must take my thoughts captive right from the start or I'll eventually give in to them. I choose to take every thought captive to the obedience of Christ and to renew my mind with God's Word. In Jesus' name I pray. Amen.

TODAY'S BIBLE READING

Proverbs 25:1-28
Theme: Relationships

DAY THIRTY-FIVE

CHOOSE TO THINK THE TRUTH

Finally, brothers, whatever is true, whatever is noble, whatever is right, whatever is pure, whatever is lovely, whatever is admirable—if anything is excellent or praiseworthy—think about such things (Philippians 4:8).

There is someone active in the world today who doesn't want you to think or believe the truth about God, yourself, or sexual purity. Paul writes, "The Spirit clearly says that in later times some will abandon the faith and follow deceiving spirits and things taught by demons" (1 Timothy 4:1).

We have counseled hundreds of young people who struggle with their thoughts or literally hear voices. In many cases the root problem has been a spiritual battle for their minds. No wonder Paul exhorts us, "Finally, brothers, whatever is true, whatever is noble, whatever is right, whatever is pure, whatever is lovely, whatever is admirable—if anything is excellent or praiseworthy—think about such things" (Philippians 4:8). What joy we would feel if we saw life from God's point of view and thought about only His thoughts!

If Satan can get us to believe a lie, he can control our lives. He is intent on destroying our view of God, ourselves, members of the opposite sex (including our mate), and the world we live in. Our problems don't just come from what we believed in the past. Paul says we are to presently and continuously take every thought captive and make it obedient to Christ (2 Corinthians 10:5).

We believe the greatest access Satan has to the church and youth group is our unwillingness to forgive those who have hurt us. This certainly has been true with the thousands of youth we have worked with. If you have been sexually abused and struggle with thoughts like "I can't forgive that person," "I hate that person," or "I don't want to forgive him; I want him to suffer as much as he made me suffer," Satan has outwitted you. He has planted his thoughts in your mind. You must renounce those schemes and choose to believe and act on the truth.

Look at 2 Corinthians 4:4: "The god of this age has blinded the minds of unbelievers, so that they cannot see the light of the gospel of the glory of Christ." The one who raises up thoughts against the knowledge of God has a field day with the sexually abused. "Where is your God now?" he taunts. "If God is love, why does He allow the innocent to suffer? If God is all-powerful, why didn't He stop that person from violating you?" Such is the smokescreen of lies that Satan uses to blind us to the truth.

Look at one more verse: "I am afraid that just as Eve was deceived by the serpent's cunning, your minds may somehow be led astray from your sincere and pure devotion to Christ" (2 Corinthians 11:3). We're concerned too, because we see so many teenagers living in bondage to those lies and wandering from devotion to Christ.

Satan is the father of lies, and he will work on our minds to destroy our concept of God and our understanding of who we are as children of God. Young people in bondage don't know who they are in Christ. That is the one common factor in every person we have helped to find freedom in Christ. Satan can't do anything about our position in Christ, but if he can get us to believe it isn't true, we will live as though it's not true, even though it is.

Satan preys on the minds of wounded teenagers—the victim of a broken home, the child of an alcoholic, someone who was sexually abused as a child, etc. Such young people are prime candidates for Satan's lies because their minds have already been pummeled with self-doubt, fear, anger, and hatred because of their circumstances. But you don't have to be the victim of a broken home or a painful childhood to be the target of the enemy's sexual temptations, accusations, and deceptions.

Don't assume that all disturbing thoughts are from Satan. We live in a sinful world with tempting images and messages all around us. You have memories of hurtful experiences which prompt thoughts contrary to the knowledge of God. Whether the thought was introduced into your mind from TV, your memory bank, Satan, or your own imagination doesn't matter much, because the answer is always the same: Choose to reject the lie and think the truth.

You can try to figure out the source of every thought, but it won't really solve the problem unless you know the solution. The answer is Christ. His truth will set you free.

Love Lessons

Satan's great power is to try to get us to believe a lie. What are some of the lies he tries to get you to believe?

Are you struggling with thoughts raised up against God, or do you frequently entertain thoughts of who you are in Christ (your identity)?

How can Satan control us if we believe his lies?

Why shouldn't we try to identity the source of every thought we have? What should we do instead?

THE LIE TO REJECT

I renounce the lie that Satan can in any way change my position in Christ.

THE TRUTH TO ACCEPT

I accept the truth that God has declared me holy and that I am now God's child. I know that no one can separate me from the love of God.

PRAYER FOR TODAY

Dear Lord, I don't want to fall for any of Satan's evil tricks. I want to be on the alert, standing guard over my heart and mind so that I'm not deceived. I know that Satan can't touch my position in Christ. But I know he will try to work on my mind to destroy my concept of You and Your love and holiness. I also know that he wants to destroy my understanding of who I am as a child of God. I choose to be in Your Word and to believe what it says about You and what it says about me as a child of God. In Jesus' name I pray. Amen.

TODAY'S BIBLE READING

Proverbs 26:1-28
Theme: Fools, sluggards, and gossips

PART EIGHT

Love That Sets You Free

Dead to Sin

What shall we say, then? Shall we go on sinning so that grace may increase? By no means! We died to sin; how can we live in it any longer? (Romans 6:1,2).

What do you believe about who you are in Christ? The Bible says of us, "As he thinks within himself, so he is" (Proverbs 23:7 NASB). Satan's deceptions and lies have destroyed a lot of people because of their lack of knowledge (Hosea 4:6). Your choice to believe God or Satan is the difference between freedom and bondage. Christians who fail to walk in victory are really showing that they have a messed-up belief system.

God sees you alive in Christ. Your soul is in union with God. This truth is one of the most crucial ideas for you to grasp! The more you understand what it means to be in Christ, the more you will experience spiritual freedom.

For example, you may see yourself as a weak and struggling Christian who just can't seem to get it together. But God sees you as His dear child, holy and blameless, with everything you need to walk in victory instead of failure. Who's right?

God is! You see, deep down inside, the real you is spiritually alive in Christ! You are forgiven, free from sin's power, united to the One who has all power. Your failure to live in victory is due in part to the fact that you have not seen yourself as God sees you. Let God open your eyes right now!

When you come to a command in the Bible, the only proper response is to obey it. But when Scripture states something that is factually true, the only proper response is to believe it. This is a simple concept, but people often get it twisted by trying to *do* something that God only expects them to *believe and accept as truth* before living accordingly by faith.

Nowhere is this more likely to occur than in Romans 6:1-11. Many Christians read this section and ask, "How do I do that?" Romans 6:1-11 is not something you can *do;* it's only something you can *believe.* But believing it will totally affect your walk by faith. It is the critical first step to finding the way of escape from sin. "What shall we say, then? Shall we go on sinning so that grace may increase? By no means! We died to sin; how can we live in it any longer?" (Romans 6:1,2).

The defeated Christian teenager asks, "How do I do that? How do I die to sin, including the sexual sins which have me bound?" The answer is, "You can't do it!" Why not? Because you have already died to sin at salvation. "We died to sin" is past tense; it has already been done. This is something you must *believe,* not something you must *do.*

"I can't be dead to sin," you may say, "because I don't feel dead to sin." You will have to set your feelings aside for a few verses, because it's what you *believe* that sets you free, not what you *feel.* God's Word is true whether you choose to believe it or not. Believing the Word of God doesn't make it true; His Word is true regardless, and therefore you must believe it even if your emotions don't cooperate. Don't try to become something you already are.

"Don't you know that all of us who were baptized into Christ Jesus were baptized into his death?" (Romans 6:3). You may still be wondering, "How do I do that?" The answer is the same: You can't do it, because you have already been baptized into Christ Jesus. It happened the moment you placed your faith in Jesus Christ as Savior and Lord. It is no good trying to seek something that the Bible tells us we already have: "We were all baptized by one Spirit into one body" (1 Corinthians 12:13). "We were" is past tense. It's done; now you just need to believe it!

LOVE LESSONS

What do you believe about who you are in Christ? Why is knowing who you are in Christ such a crucial issue?

What happens if you see yourself as a weak and struggling Christian who just can't seem to get it together?

What does the Bible mean when it says that we are dead to sin?

Does the fact that we are dead to sin give us a license to commit sins? Explain.

THE LIE TO REJECT

I renounce the lie of Satan that I am still alive to sin.

THE TRUTH TO ACCEPT

I accept the truth that I am now dead to sin and alive in Christ Jesus.

Prayer for Today

Dear Lord, Thank You for the position that I now have in Christ Jesus. I know that the law was powerless to save me from my sin but Christ fulfilled the law and set me free from sin and bondage by dying for me on the cross. I know that sin is still present in the world but that I am under no obligation to obey its empty calls because I am dead to sin and have new life in Christ. In Jesus' name I pray. Amen.

Today's Bible Reading

Proverbs 27:1-27
Theme: Life

YOU HAVE NEW LIFE

We were therefore buried with him through baptism into death in order that, just as Christ was raised from the dead through the glory of the Father, we too may live a new life. If we have been united with him like this in his death, we will certainly also be united with him in his resurrection" (Romans 6:4,5).

Have we been united with Christ? Absolutely! "If we have been united with him" can literally be read: "If we have become united with Him in the likeness of His death—and we certainly have—we shall also be united with Him in the likeness of His resurrection."

You cannot identify with the death and burial of Christ without also identifying with His resurrection and ascension. You will live in defeat if you believe only half the gospel. You have died with Christ, and you have been raised with Him and seated in the heavenlies (Ephesians 2:6). From this position you have the authority and power you need to live the Christian life.

Every child of God is spiritually alive and therefore "in Christ." Paul clearly identifies every believer, young or old, as "in Christ":

- In His death (Romans 6:3,6; Galatians 2:20; Colossians 3:1-3).
- In His burial (Romans 6:4).

- In His resurrection (Romans 6:5,8,11).
- In His ascension (Ephesians 2:6).
- In His life (Romans 5:10,11).
- In His power (Ephesians 1:19,20).
- In His inheritance (Romans 8:16,17; Ephesians 1:11,12).

Jesus didn't come only to die for our sins; He also came that we might have life (John 10:10). We celebrate the resurrection of Jesus Christ on Easter, not just His death on Good Friday. It is the *resurrected life of Christ* that God has given to us. Notice how Paul develops this truth in Romans 5:8-11: "God demonstrates his own love for us in this: While we were still sinners, Christ died for us" (verse 8).

Isn't that great? God loves you! But is that all? No! "Since we have now been justified by his blood, how much more shall we be saved from God's wrath through him!" (verse 9).

Isn't that great? You're not going to hell! But is that all? No! "For if, when we were God's enemies, we were reconciled to him through the death of his Son, how much more, having been reconciled, shall we be saved through his life!" (verse 10).

Isn't that great? You have been saved by His life! Eternal life isn't something you get when you die; you are alive in Christ right now. But is that all? No! "Not only is this so, but we also rejoice in God through our Lord Jesus Christ, through whom we have now received reconciliation (peace)" (verse 11). This peaceful union assures us that our souls are in union with God, which is what it means to be spiritually alive.

Are you beginning to see a glimmer of hope for overcoming sin? You should be, because you have already died to it and been raised to new and victorious life in Christ!

"For we know that our old self was crucified with him so that the body of sin might be done away with, that we should no longer be slaves to sin" (Romans 6:6). The verse does not say "we do" but "we know." Your old self was crucified when Christ was crucified. The only proper response to this truth is to believe it. Many young people are desperately trying to put to death the old self with all its tendencies to sin, but they can't do it. Why not? Because it is already dead! You cannot do what God alone has already done for you.

Christians who continually fail in their Christian walk begin to question incorrectly, "What experience must I have in order for me to live victoriously?" There is none. The only experience that was necessary for this verse to be true occurred nearly 2000 years ago on the cross. And the only way we can enter into that experience today is by faith. We can't save ourselves, and we can't by human effort overcome the penalty of death or the power of sin. Only God can do that for us, and He has already done it.

We don't live obediently because we hope that someday God may accept us. *We are already accepted by God*, so we live obediently. It is not what we *do* that determines who we are; *it is who we are and what we believe that determines what we do.*

When Jesus went to the cross, all the sins of the world were laid upon Him. When they nailed those spikes into His hands and feet, all the sins of the world were upon Him. But when He was raised from the dead, there were no sins at all upon Him. They stayed in the grave. As He sits at the right hand of the Father today, there are no sins upon Him. He has triumphed over sin and death. And since you are in Him, you are also dead to sin.

Many teenagers accept the truth that Christ died for the sins they have already committed. But what about the sins they will commit in the future? When Christ died for *all* your sins, how many of your sins were then future? All of them, of course! This is not a license to sin, which leads to bondage, but a marvelous truth on which to stand against Satan's accusations. It is something we must know in order to live free in Christ.

LOVE LESSONS

How have we been united with Christ?

Of all the ways that we are united with Christ, which one excites you the most? Why?

What happened to the old you (your old self) when you came to Christ?

What happens to the sins we commit after we accept Christ?

THE LIE TO REJECT

I renounce the lie of Satan that I am not united with Christ.

THE TRUTH TO ACCEPT

I accept the truth that God has united me with Christ and that I now belong to Him.

Prayer for Today

Dear Lord, thank You that I am united with Christ, and that I have been raised with Him and seated in the heavenlies (Ephesians 2:6). Thank You that I am a child of God and spiritually alive and therefore "in Christ." Thank You for this position of authority and power. I know You have given me all that I need to live the successful Christian life. I choose to consider myself dead to sin and alive to You. I choose to walk in Your ways and do Your will. In Jesus' name I pray. Amen.

Today's Bible Reading

Proverbs 28:1-28
Theme: Wealth

Strongholds in the Mind

I pray also that the eyes of your heart may be en-lightened in order that you may know the hope to which he has called you, the riches of his glorious inheritance in the saints, and his incomparably great power for us who believe (Ephesians 1:18,19).

A stronghold is an established, habitual pattern of thinking and behaving against which a person is virtually powerless to choose or act. Strongholds form in two ways, often beginning early in life.

The first kind forms through the experiences in our lives, such as families, friends, churches, neighborhoods, jobs, etc. As children, our attitudes and actions were partially shaped by these influences. For example, friends who shared their pornographic magazines with you may have encouraged you into a fascination with or bondage to pornography. Or if sexual abuses occurred, those experiences have influenced your thinking and behavior.

But environment isn't the only thing that determines how we develop. Two children can be raised in the same home by the same parents, eat the same food, play with the same friends, and attend the same church but still respond differently to life. We are individually created expressions of God's workmanship (Psalm 139:13,14; Ephesians 2:10). Despite having the same parents and upbringing, our particular differences make our responses to the world around us unique.

The second great contributor to the development of strongholds in our minds is traumatic experiences. Whereas other experiences come into our minds over time, one traumatic experience can be instantly burned into our memory because of its intensity. For example, one bad encounter with a nest of hornets may leave a child with a deep fear of all flying, stinging insects as an adult.

As we struggle to reprogram our minds against the negative input of past experiences, we are also confronted daily with an ungodly world system. Paul warned us, "Do not conform any longer to the pattern of this world" (Romans 12:2). As Christians we are not immune to worldly values; we can allow them to affect our thinking and behavior. But Paul insisted, "Don't let them influence you!" He also instructed, "See to it that no one takes you captive through hollow and deceptive philosophy, which depends on human tradition and the basic principles of this world rather than on Christ" (Colossians 2:8).

Since we live in this world, we will continuously face the temptation to conform to it. It is not a sin to be tempted. Remember, Christ was "tempted in every way, just as we are—yet was without sin" (Hebrews 4:15). We sin when we consciously choose to give in to temptation.

All temptation is an attempt by Satan to get us to live our lives without God, to walk according to the flesh rather than according to the Spirit (see Galatians 5:16-23). Satan knows exactly which buttons to push when tempting us. He knows our weaknesses and our family history.

Each temptation begins with a seed thought planted in our minds by the world, the flesh, or the devil himself. Since we live in Satan's world, we must learn how to stand against the temptations he throws at us. Since sex is used in the media to entertain and to sell everything from beer to deodorant to toothpaste to cars, we are constantly bombarded with seed thoughts perverting God's plan for sex. Many people can be tempted to sexual sin without much prompting from the external world, because they have programmed so much junk into their minds through TV, movies, books, and magazines. They can fantasize for years without leaving their homes.

That's why sexual strongholds are so difficult to overcome. Once they are formed in the mind, the mental pictures are there for instant recall. An alcoholic can't get drunk by fantasizing about a bottle. A drug addict can't get high by imagining himself snorting cocaine. A habitual overeater isn't soothed thinking about a giant chocolate cake. But some victims of sexual bondage can get a rush or a high without any new pictures in the mind to draw from. Of course, pornography and illicit sexual activities serve to reinforce and strengthen sexual strongholds.

If we continue to act on wrong choices when we are tempted, a habit can be formed in about six weeks. If the habit goes on, a stronghold will be developed in the mind.

Strongholds are mental habit patterns that have been burned into our minds over time or by the intensity of traumatic experiences.

LOVE LESSONS

Explain in your own words what a stronghold is.

How do strongholds form?

Take some time now and ask the Lord to reveal to your mind if there are any strongholds in your life.

If there is a stronghold in your life, what was the first experience that opened the door to this bad habit? Take some time and renounce that event and the stronghold.

Further help can be found in the Steps to Freedom, available from Freedom in Christ Youth Ministries.

THE LIE TO REJECT

I renounce the lie of Satan that I am condemned to live a life of bondage.

THE TRUTH TO ACCEPT

I accept the truth that God has set me free from the sins of past and that I can choose to walk free as a child of God when I confess and renounce my sin.

PRAYER FOR TODAY

Dear Lord, You see everything I have ever done, yet You still love me. I give You permission to reveal to my mind any stronghold or bad habit that I have allowed to control my life. I want to walk free and not let any sin or destructive habit keep me from doing Your will. I want to experience Your blessing and peace. In Jesus' name I pray. Amen.

TODAY'S BIBLE READING

Proverbs 29:1-27
Theme: Stubbornness

DESTROYING THE DEVIL'S WORK

The reason the Son of God appeared was to destroy the devil's work. No one who is born of God will continue to sin, because God's seed remains in him (1 John 3:8,9).

You may know about God's plan of sexual purity and even agree with it. But, try as you might, you can't conform to it.

If God's Word so clearly and strongly commands people not to live in sexual bondage, why don't we just obey God and stop doing what He forbids? Because merely telling people that they are doing wrong doesn't give them the power to stop doing it. Paul declared, "If a law had been given that could impart life, then righteousness would certainly have come by the law" (Galatians 3:21). The law is powerless to take away the problem and give life. Something more is needed.

Even more discouraging is Paul's statement, "The sinful passions aroused by the law were at work in our bodies" (Romans 7:5). The law not only can't help us do right but it actually has the capacity to provoke what it is trying to prohibit. Forbidden fruit always appears more desirable. Laying down the law does not remove sinful passions. The abstinence message alone doesn't work; the core problem is the basic *nature* of people, not their *behavior*.

Trying to live a righteous life on the outside when we are not righteous inside will only result in us becoming "whitewashed tombs, which look beautiful on the outside but on the inside are full of dead men's bones and everything unclean" (Matthew 23:27). The focus must be on what is *inside*: "From within, out of men's hearts, come evil thoughts, sexual immorality, theft, murder, adultery, greed, malice, deceit, lewdness, envy, slander, arrogance, and folly. All these evils come from inside and make a man 'unclean'" (Mark 7:21-23).

If trying harder to break the bonds of lustful thoughts and behavior and to live in sexual purity doesn't work, what will? Two verses in the Bible state what must happen in order for us to live righteously in Christ: "The reason the Son of God appeared was to destroy the devil's work. No one who is born of God will continue to sin, because God's seed remains in him" (1 John 3:8,9). If you are going to be set free from sexual bondage and walk in that freedom, your basic nature must be changed, and you must have a means for overcoming the evil one.

For those of us who are Christians, these things have already been done. God has made us partakers of His divine nature (2 Peter 1:4) and has provided a way for us to live in victory over sin and Satan.

Before Christ, we were dead in our sins and subject to the control of Satan. But a change took place at salvation. Paul wrote, "You were once darkness, but now you are light in the Lord" (Ephesians 5:8). Our old nature in Adam was darkness; our new nature in Christ is light. We have been transformed at the core of our being. We are no longer "in the flesh"; we are "in Christ." Paul wrote, "Those who are in the flesh cannot please God. However, you are not in the flesh but in the Spirit, if indeed the Spirit of God dwells in you" (Romans 8:8,9 NASB).

Before we became Christians we were under the rule of the god of this world, Satan. But at salvation God "rescued us from the dominion of darkness and brought us into the kingdom of the Son he loves, in whom we have redemption, the forgiveness of sins" (Colossians 1:13,14). We no longer have to obey the evil prompting of the world, the flesh, and the devil. We "have been given fullness in Christ, who is the head over every power and authority" (Colossians 2:10). We are free to obey God and to walk in righteousness and purity.

There is no way we can fix the failure and sin of the past, but by the grace of God we can be free from it. God's Word promises, "If anyone is in Christ, he is a new creation; the old has gone, the new has come!" (2 Corinthians 5:17). Furthermore, we are seated with Christ in the heavenlies, far above Satan's authority (Ephesians 2:4-6; Colossians 2:10,11), paving the way for us to live in victory and freedom over sin and bondage. But we also have a responsibility: We must believe the truth of who we are in Christ and change how we walk as children of God to conform to what is true.

We already share in Christ's rich inheritance, and we already have the power to live victoriously in Christ. God has provided these glorious benefits for us. The problem for most Christians struggling in bondage is that they just don't see it.

LOVE LESSONS

Why can't we just obey God and stop doing what He forbids?

Why is the law powerless to take away the problem of sin?

What happens when we try to live a righteous life on the outside when we are not righteous inside?

What two things have to occur for every Christian so he or she can overcome the evil one?

THE LIE TO REJECT

I renounce the lie of Satan that trying harder or obeying the law can set me free.

THE TRUTH TO ACCEPT

I accept the truth that God has already set me free from sin by making me a partaker of His divine nature. I am a new creature in Christ.

PRAYER FOR TODAY

Dear Lord, thank You that my nature has been changed, and that You overcame the evil one through Christ's death, burial, and resurrection. I know now that I too can overcome the evil one because of my position in Christ. I'm Your child, a partaker of Your divine nature (2 Peter 1:4). You provided a way for me to live in victory over sin and Satan. In Jesus' name I pray. Amen.

TODAY'S BIBLE READING

Proverbs 30:1-33
Theme: Personal words

DAY FORTY

BREAKING THE STRONGHOLDS

If anyone is in Christ, he is a new creation; the old has gone, the new has come! (2 Corinthians 5:17).

Can strongholds of sexual bondage in the mind be broken? Yes! If our minds have been programmed wrongly, they can be reprogrammed. Will this take time? Yes, it will take the rest of our lives to fully renew our minds and to fully develop our character. We will never be completely perfect in our understanding on this earth, nor will our character be as perfect as Christ's, but this is what we go after.

Christian growth can't take place unless we are free in Christ. When people aren't free in Christ they go from book to book, from youth pastor to youth pastor, and from counselor to counselor, but nothing seems to work. Watch how fast they can grow, however, when they are free in Christ!

Think of your polluted mind as a 44-ounce cup filled to the top with Dr. Pepper. Sitting beside the Dr. Pepper is a huge bowl of crystal-clear ice, which represents the Word of God. Your goal is to purify the contents in the cup by adding ice cubes to it. Every cube displaces some of the pop and dilutes the rest, making it a little purer. You can only put in one or two cubes a day, so the process seems futile at first. But over the course of time the water begins to look less and less polluted and the taste and smell of Dr. Pepper is getting weaker. The process continues to work provided you don't add more Dr. Pepper to the cup.

Paul writes, "Let the peace of Christ rule in your hearts, since as members of one body you were called to peace. And be thankful" (Colossians 3:15). How do we rid ourselves of evil thoughts, purify our mind, and allow the peace of Christ to reign within us?

The answer is found in Colossians 3:16: "Let the word of Christ dwell in you richly." Also, "How can a young man keep his way pure? By living according to your word. I seek you with all my heart; do not let me stray from your commands. I have hidden your word in my heart that I might not sin against you" (Psalm 119:9-11). Just trying to stop thinking bad thoughts won't work. We must fill our minds with the crystal-clear Word of God. God has no other plan.

You may find that winning the battle for your mind is initially a two-steps-forward, one-step-back process as you take on the world, the flesh, and the devil. But gradually it will become three steps forward, one step back, then four and five steps forward as you learn to take every thought captive and make it obedient to Christ. You may despair with all your steps backward, but God won't give up on you. Remember, your sins are already forgiven. You only need to fight for your own personal victory over sin. This is a winnable war because you are alive in Christ and dead to sin. The bigger battle has already been won by Christ.

Freedom to be all that God has called you to be is the greatest blessing in this present life. This freedom is worth fighting for. As you learn more about who you are as a child of God and about the nature of the battle waging for your mind, the process gets easier. Eventually it is 20 steps forward and one back, and finally the steps are all forward, with only an occasional slip in the battle for the mind.

Love Lessons

What needs to happen in our lives for Christian growth to take place?

How do we rid ourselves of evil thoughts, purify our mind, and allow the peace of Christ to reign?

Is there any area of your life where you're not experiencing God's freedom? If so, why not confess and renounce it right now!

The Lie to Reject

I renounce the lie of Satan that strongholds cannot be broken.

The Truth to Accept

I accept the truth that God has already set me free through Christ's death, burial, and resurrection.

Prayer for Today

Dear Lord, thank You for Your great love for me. I know that nothing I could ever do could change Your love for me. I know that if I choose the road of freedom, it will bring peace. I want to give my life to You because I love You, and not just because Your ways bring peace. Lord, words just can't express how much I truly love You. How can I ever begin to thank You for all the things You have done for me? The position You have given me in Christ is so awesome. I still don't understand it all. Lord, help me to understand the depth of who I am in You. I choose to walk free and to serve and worship You. In Jesus' name I pray. Amen.

TODAY'S BIBLE READING

Proverbs 31:1-31
Theme: A good wife

Notes

Part One: Ultimate Love

1. *Webster's Dictionary* (Ashland, OH: Landall's, 1993), p. 156.
2. Brennan Manning, *The Ragamuffin Gospel* (Sisters, OR: Multnomah Books, 1990), pp. 31-32.
3. Wayne Rice, *Hot Illustrations for Youth Talks* (Zondervan Publishing House, 1994, by Youth Specialties Inc., El Cajon, CA, adapted from "Bear in the Cave"), pp. 26-27.

Part Two: God's Chosen Ones

1. Wayne Rice, *Hot Illustrations for Youth Talks* (Zondervan Publishing House, 1994, by Youth Specialties Inc., El Cajon, CA, "Lost Dog"), p. 148.

Part Three: Loving God

1. Wayne Rice, *Hot Illustrations for Youth Talks* (Zondervan Publishing House, 1994, by Youth Specialties Inc., El Cajon, CA, "Alexander the Great"), pp. 18-19.
2. Wayne Rice, *Hot Illustrations for Youth Talks* (Zondervan Publishing House, 1994, by Youth Specialties Inc., El Cajon, CA, "The Kiss"), p. 131.
3. J. K. Summerhill.

Part Four: Love and Friendships

1. Wayne Rice, *Hot Illustrations for Youth Talks* (Zondervan Publishing House, 1994, by Youth Specialties Inc., El Cajon, CA, "What Life?"), p. 221.

Part Five: Love and Dating

1. Wayne Rice, *Hot Illustrations for Youth Talks* (Zondervan Publishing House, 1994, by Youth Specialties Inc., El Cajon, CA, "Blind Date"), p. 38.

Part Six: Love and Sex

1. Adapted from Gordon MacDonald, *Rebuilding Your Broken World* (Nashville, TN: Oliver Nelson Publishers, 1988), p. 150.
2. Joe McIlaney, *Sexuality and Sexually Transmitted Diseases* (Grand Rapids, MI: Baker Book House, 1990), p. 14.
3. C.S. Lewis, *The Lion, the Witch and the Wardrobe* (New York, NY: Macmillan Publishing Company, 1950), p. 33.
4. Adapted from Gordon MacDonald, *Rebuilding Your Broken World* (Nashville, TN: Oliver Nelson Publishers, 1988), p. 162.

Part Seven: Love and the Second Chance

1. Kay Arthur, *Lord I Want to Know You* (Multnomah Books, 1991), pp. 47-48.

For more information about friendships, dating, and relationships or more information about breaking sexual bondages, check out Neil and Dave's book *Purity Under Pressure*. This book contains the Steps to Freedom and is a more detailed study of sexual pressures and how to walk free in Christ.

"Understanding your identity in Christ is
absolutely essential to your success at living
the victorious Christian life!"

Who am I?

I am accepted ...

John 1:12	I am God's child.
John 15:15	I am Christ's friend.
Rom. 5:1	I have been justified.
1 Cor. 6:17	I am united with the Lord, and I am one spirit with Him.
1 Cor. 6:19,20	I have been bought with a price. I belong to God.
1 Cor. 12:27	I am a member of Christ's body.
Eph. 1:1	I am a saint.
Eph. 1:5	I have been adopted as God's child.
Eph. 2:18	I have direct access to God through the Holy Spirit.
Col. 1:14	I have been redeemed and forgiven of all my sins.
Col. 2:10	I am complete in Christ.

I am secure ...

Rom. 8:1,2	I am free forever from condemnation.
Rom. 8:28	I am assured that all things work together for good.
Rom. 8:31f	I am free from any condemning charges against me.
Rom. 8:35f	I cannot be separated from the love of God.
2 Cor. 1:21,22	I have been established, anointed, and sealed by God.
Col. 3:3	I am hidden with Christ in God.
Phil. 1:6	I am confident that the good work that God has begun in me will be perfected.
Phil. 3:20	I am a citizen of heaven.
2 Tim. 1:7	I have not been given a spirit of fear but of power, love, and a sound mind.
Heb. 4:16	I can find grace and mercy in time of need.
1 John 5:18	I am born of God, and the evil one cannot touch me.

I am significant ...

Matt. 5:13,14	I am the salt and light of the earth.
John 15:1,5	I am a branch of the true vine, a channel of His life.
Acts 1:8	I am a personal witness of Christ's.
1 Cor. 3:16	I am God's temple.
2 Cor. 5:17f	I am a minister of reconciliation for God.
2 Cor. 6:1	I am God's coworker (1 Cor. 3:9).
Eph. 2:6	I am seated with Christ in the heavenly realm.
Eph. 2:10	I am God's workmanship.
Eph. 3:12	I may approach God with freedom and confidence.
Phil. 4:13	I can do all things through Christ who strengthens me.

(From "Living Free in Christ" by Dr. Neil Anderson)

Other Books by Neil and Dave

Bondage Breaker, Youth Edition
Bondage Breaker, Youth Edition Study Guide
Stomping Out the Darkness
Stomping Out the Darkness, Study Guide
Busting Free, Youth Curriculum

Freedom in Christ 4 Teens

Devotional Series

Extreme Faith
by Neil T. Anderson and Dave Park

Reality Check
by Neil T. Anderson and Rich Miller

Other Youth Resources from Freedom in Christ

To My Dear Slimeball
by Rich Miller

Know Him, No Fear
by Rich Miller and Neil Anderson

Freedom in Christ Youth Conferences

Stomping Out the Darkness
For high school and junior high students

Setting Your Youth Free
For adults who serve youth

Purity Under Pressure
For high school and junior high students

For more information about having a
Freedom in Christ youth event in your area, call or write:

Freedom in Christ Youth Ministries
491 E. Lambert Road
La Habra, CA 90631
(310) 691-9128